The Political Economy of the Asia Pacific

Series editor

Vinod K. Aggarwal

More information about this series at http://www.springer.com/series/7840

Seungjoo Lee • Sang-young Rhyu

The Political Economy of Change and Continuity in Korea

Twenty Years after the Crisis

Springer

Seungjoo Lee
Chung-Ang University
Dongjak-gu, Seoul, Korea (Republic of)

Sang-young Rhyu
Yonsei University
Seodaemoon-gu, Seoul, Korea (Republic of)

ISSN 1866-6507 ISSN 1866-6515 (electronic)
The Political Economy of the Asia Pacific
ISBN 978-3-319-71451-6 ISBN 978-3-319-71453-0 (eBook)
https://doi.org/10.1007/978-3-319-71453-0

Library of Congress Control Number: 2017963867

Printed on acid-free paper

This Springer imprint is published by the registered company Springer Nature Switzerland AG.
The registered company address is: Gewerbestrasse 11, 6330 Cham, Switzerland

Preface

Twenty years has passed since South Korea fell victim to the Asian financial crisis. Although Korea officially announced in 1999 that it overcame the crisis to repay the IMF loans, it still suffered from the specter of the crisis. The crisis profoundly changed the nature of the Korean political economy, igniting numerous discussions and debates. What has changed in the political economy in Korea since the crisis? How did such changes proceed? Numerous scholars argued that the crisis served as a catalyst in transforming the political economy in Korea, but failed to reach a general consensus on the nature of the transformation and the consequences the crisis left. It was because the Korean political economy did not take unidirectional changes to neoliberalism, departing away from the traditional developmentalism. In contrast to conventional wisdom, we present a novel interpretation of the political economy in Korea since the crisis. We particularly shed light on the fact that the Korean political economy demonstrated the dual dynamics of changes and continuity in the process of institutional transformation.

To explore this unique phenomenon, we had to go through numerous discussions. The dual dynamics resulted from a variety of factors: discrepancy between formal structures and informal networks, changing government-business relations, and path-dependent nature of institutional change. We attempted to show the way in which the dual dynamics has played out in making institutional transition in important areas such as chaebol reform, the privatization of public corporations, and the impact of informal networks on newly formed institutions. The dual dynamics also emerged in the process of industrial restructuring such as the IT and aircraft industries.

Generous institutional support helped us explore the primary nature of the transformative process in the Korean political economy. The Kim Dae-jung Presidential Library and Museum, Yonsei University, was instrumental in bringing our long intellectual effort to fruition. Also, this book would not have been complete without Lorraine Klimowich's patience and utmost professionalism.

Dongjak-gu, Seoul, Korea (Republic of) — Seungjoo Lee
Seodaemoon-gu, Seoul, Korea (Republic of) — Sang-young Rhyu

Contents

Chapter 1
Introduction: Change and Continuity in Institutional Transformation in Korea

The political economy in South Korea (hereafter Korea) has dramatically transformed since the Asian financial crisis in 1997. Interestingly, since the crisis, the political economy of Korea has displayed two diametrically opposed features (Park 2015). One the one hand, the institutional foundations that spearheaded high economic growth until the 1980s eroded in the face of the forces of globalization ushered in by the crisis (Pirie 2006, 2012; Moon and Chung 2014). It seems that under the exponentially increasing complexity of the world economy, the Korean government is no longer able to provide a strategic guidance for the national economy, rapidly converging into the Anglo-American model of political economy. The track record of liberalization measures such as financial liberalization, corporate governance reform, and labor reform suggests that the empirical basis of these arguments is robust.

On the other hand, a close look into the economic reform process in Korea demonstrates that in meeting these new challenges the Korean political economy has showed a great deal of adaptive capability (Lim 2008; Kim 2013; Kalinowski 2015). In this regard, the main thrust of the Korean political economy is kept intact rather than converging into the Anglo-American model. In the aftermath of the economic crisis, the restructuring of Korean political economy was implemented not through the retreat of the state but by active state intervention. For example, the IT industry went through strategic restructuring that aimed to introduce competition among domestic companies before opening up the market to foreign firms (Lee 2004).

Why and how do the two different features – convergence into the Anglo-American model and the state-led strategic restructuring of industries – coexist in Korea? That is, the political economy of Korea since the Asian financial crisis has shown the dual dynamics of change and continuity. To answer this question, we argue that under the crisis situation, ideological shift within the political leadership and institutional transformation of the Korean state combined to determine this unique outcome.

S. Lee and S. Rhyu, *The Political Economy of Change and Continuity in Korea*,
The Political Economy of the Asia Pacific, https://doi.org/10.1007/978-3-319-71453-0_1

To unravel the peculiar nature of the political economy in Korea, we will identify major factors that contributed to the dual dynamics of change and continuity in Korea: external pressures, ideological shift in political leadership, and the pivotal role of the Korean government. Also, we will examine the way in which these factors interacted with each other to (re)shape the evolutionary path of the Korean political economy. First, rampant bilateral (the U.S.) and multilateral (the IMF) pressures offered a broad contour of the future path of changes in Korea. In the face of such pressures, the Korean government was forced to carry out the so-called neoliberal reform such as market opening, privatization, and labor reforms.[1] However, while suffering from it, the Korean government strategically utilized the pressure to enhance its capability vis-à-vis domestic interest groups and successfully preempted their potential opposition.

Second, the Korean political economy made a fundamental shift toward liberalization departing from the past legacies of developmentalism, while the Korean government attempted to find a new activist role (Yoon 2009). The Korean government at the center of this dynamics of change and continuity ambitiously introduced financial and corporate governance reform while it attempted to play a pivotal role in reshaping individual industrial sectors such as IT and aerospace. In this regard, the reform process in Korea was essentially state-led, in which the Korean government has largely replicated the past practices of state intervention in economic affairs.

Third, the dual dynamics of change and continuity is also found in institutional re-building. The Korean government undertook a major institutional restructuring reflecting the emerging domestic and external changes (Shin and Chang 2003). However, the reformulation of institutions was designed to minimize functional mismatch between government's authority and new business realities. This change ultimately made possible for the Korean government to make decisions in a coherent and timely manner. The Korean government carefully designed the reform process and significantly influenced the final outcome. In this process, the Korean government found a new activist role for itself at a time when critics of developmental state urged to reduce state intervention in the economy.

1.1 The Asian Financial Crisis and the Korean Development Model at a Crossroads

The Asian financial crisis was not just an economic crisis but a political and social crisis in that it served as a catalyst that spurred economic, political, and social changes (MacIntyre et al. 2008). A structural perspective finds the primary cause of the Korean development model in the vulnerability of the high-debt model and

[1] By contrast, Thurbon argues that the political leadership's ambition dictated the Korean government's for ill-designed and reckless liberalization in the pre-crisis period, which ultimately became structural causes of the crisis (Thurbon 2001).

problems associated with crony capitalism (Krugman 1998; Hughes 1999). One can find structural problems of the Korean development model in capital accumulation and mobilization for industrialization. During the high growth period, *chaebols* could manage high debt-to-equity ratio, about 400% on average, as long as they could maintain profitability to redeem the debt (Wade and Veneroso 1998). The high-debt model could be maintained because the Korean government took advantage of the high debt as a leverage to deal with private companies during the high-growth period. However, the high-debt model revealed the structural constraints as many of chaebols ran into problems stemming from excessive investment and production.

Crony capitalism, which ignited intense discussions and debates in the aftermath of the Asian financial crisis, is also considered responsible for the structural problems of the Korean development model (Kim and Lim 2000). Mainly drawing on transaction cost theory, this view takes a political economy approach. David Kang (2002) argues that although corruption between government and business did exist during the high-growth period, it did not reach to the extent to disrupt economic growth because the Korean government and chaebol could balance each other. However, after the democratic transition, the Korean government became vulnerable to chaebol's lobby because the balance gradually shifted to chaebol as the demand for political contribution exponentially increased (Kang 2002).

Lee et al. (2002) offers a noble perspective distinct from Kang's explanation. A profound change in government-business relations resulted in chaebol-dominant economic system, which is a main culprit of the Asian financial crisis. As its dependence on financial mobilization mediated by the government lowered, chaebol could gradually decompose the hierarchical relationship to increase its influence on the Korean government, paving the way for crony capitalism in Korea (Lee et al. 2002).

While the Asian financial crisis revealed structural problems built in the Korean development model that had exorbitantly relied on high-debts, it also resulted from a series of policy mistakes committed by the Korean government such as hasty break-up of the Korean development model, the lack of institutional transition strategy, and excessive liberalization (Krugman 1997; Shin and Chang 2003). In particular, the malfunction of the Korean model inherently stemmed from the Korea's push for financial liberalization in the early 1990s. The Kim Young-sam government introduced liberalization measures in the financial sector as it aspired to be a member of OECD (Weiss 2000). Systemic instability dramatically heightened in the traditional model of development because the tightly coupled institutional elements began to unravel without sophisticated plans.

In contrast to the above explanations, a number of studies shed light on external factors that caused the fundamental changes in the Korean model of development. In the outbreak of the Asian financial crisis, Wall Street-Treasury-IMF complex precipitated the dissolution of the Korean model by asking the Korean government to implement stringent fiscal policy and financial liberalization in return for the IMF rescue loan (Wade and Veneroso 1998). In this view, the implementation of the IMF program was a watershed in turning to neoliberal model of development away from developmentalism, because both short-term policy measures to cope with the financial crisis as well as long-term reform programs included neoliberal elements (Yoon 2009). Because the short-term policy recommendations did aim to drive out companies suffering from high debt-to-equity ratio, they were considered a dire challenge to the existing system. Moreover, the structural and institutional reform constituted of financial reform, corporate reform, public sector reform, and labor reform included neoliberal elements such as liberalization, changes in corporate governance, increase in labor flexibility, and privatization (Ji 2009; Um et al. 2014). The shift to neoliberalism was made in the context of embracing the IMF programs (Camdessus 1999).

1.2 Changes in Developmentalism and Institutional Transition

Since the Asian financial crisis in 1997, various attempts were made to explain whether the Korean development model entered into a new stage. External shocks such as the Asian financial crisis may serve as a catalyst (MacIntyre et al. 2008), because it is not an easy task to overhaul the traditional model of development that had been created and maintained since the early 1960s. Therefore, it is generally acknowledged that the Korean political economy went through substantial modification, but there still exist wide gaps in assessing the way in which the Korean development model has completely unraveled since the crisis. The debates center around the issue of 'continuity and change.' From the perspective of discontinuity, a number of scholars stress that the Korean development model has undergone a qualitative change moving away from the development model (Lee et al. 2002).

By contrast, other scholars understand the primary nature of the political economy that has proceeded for the last two decades from the perspective of continuity. Whereas this perspective does not deny that Korea was forced to embrace various elements of the neoliberal model, it posits that despite such changes, Korea still could maintain core elements of the existing development model. In particular, it highlights that the Korean regime did not abandon the government's active role of industrial promotion even under the neoliberal reforms. Furthermore, the modification of regulatory system, an intrinsic element of neoliberalism, brought about unintended effects of strengthening the Korean government's role.

For example, the Kim Dae-jung government in the midst of the Asian financial crisis promoted IT industry as a new growth engine by providing intensive supportive measures, created the Financial Supervisory Service (FSS) to tighten regulation of the financial industry that was an immediate cause of the crisis, and strengthened the Fair Trade Commission (FTC) to invigorate market competition. Because these changes involved the expansion of the government's role, Korea hardly derailed from the existing development model. Also, the attempts to eradicate crony capitalism that was identified as a root cause of the crisis were substantially compromised, resulting in sectoral diversification (Ha 2012).

While recognizing that the existing debates tend to focus on one aspect of the change, we attempt to demonstrate the way in which developmentalism and neoliberalism have combined in the post-crisis period in Korea. First, there is substantial discrepancy between policy ideas as guiding principles of the economy and policy practices in reality. The Korean government still possesses capacity and policy tools although neoliberal ideas greatly diffused within the policy circle (Lim 2008; Kalinowski 2015). The Korean government's operation and management style remained unchanged when it comes down to the implementation. Korea selectively introduced neoliberal ideas as policy tools while maintaining core goals of the developmental state. Despite selective adoption of neoliberal policies, Korea did not abandon international competitiveness as an essential goal. As a result, policy practices that had underpinned developmentalism are still at work in an informal way (Rhyu and Lee 2006; Stubbs 2009).

Second, the Korean political economy made institutional transitions by embracing neoliberal paradigm of economic management, which was a rational response to changing domestic and international environments. However, the Korean government made such a decision to assist private companies to compete in the world market where international competition has intensified, rather than to introduce a full-scale market-led economic government in the Korean economy. Neoliberal policies were not a driver of institutional transition, but a means to achieve the mercantilist goal of winning international competition. Paradoxically, the Korean government intermittently intervened in the market to implement neoliberal policies (Stubbs 2009), demonstrating path-dependent nature of changes. Because Korea had to seek changes under the shadow of developmentalism even after catch-up was completed, institutional transition tended to focus on continuity rather than the break-up of the past system of development (Woo 1999, xii).

Whereas this view aptly captures the nature of changes, it does not offer an analytical framework that can explain how path dependence has played out in the post-crisis period in Korea. First, the path dependence argument should demonstrate that although there existed multiple choices actor could choose from. Second, it should show how the dynamics of path dependence encourages the actors to seek changes within the contour of the existing status-quo. In order to demonstrate this process, scholars of path dependence employ various mechanisms such as externality, lock-in, self-reinforcing, and feedback (Pierson 1999; Mahoney 2000).

1.3 Dynamic Interaction Between Developmentalism and Neoliberalism

It is of paramount importance to explain how and why the combination of developmentalism and neoliberalism proceeded in the evolution of the Korean model of development. For a comprehensive overview of interplay between developmentalism and neoliberalism in Korea, see Lee (2018). Without specifying the mechanism and process, either the developmentalism thesis or the neoliberalism thesis is unsubstantiated and lacks empirical analysis. In the post-crisis period, Korea got involved in seemingly contradictory dynamics where developmentalism and neoliberalism coexist. In the process of institutional transition to neoliberalism, elements of developmentalism was largely maintained rather than completely scrapped (Yang 2005). This dynamics dictated the nature and scope of changes in the post-crisis Korea.

From the perspective of developmentalism, the Korean government still carries out tasks of promoting new growth industry and shedding off industries in decline (Wade 1990). The case of the IT industry is a good case that demonstrates the dynamics of coexistence (Lee and Park 2010). Targeting the IT industry as a candidate for industrial upgrading in the wake of the Asian financial crisis, the Kim Dae-jung government embarked on institutional changes that could effectively support the development of the IT industry. In this process, the Kim Dae-jung government displayed a developmentalist posture, injecting massive financial resources with relatively low-interest rates in the IT industry, which was a classic case of "setting the relative prices wrong" (Amsden 1989). Thanks to the government support, the IT industry could wean away from foreign technologies to emerge as a leading export industry in Korea (Byon et al. 2002).

Nonetheless, the new model of political economy is distinctive from the development model of the high-growth period, particularly in terms of government-business relations. While taking the initiative for the development of the IT industry, the Korean government shifted to indirect and sophisticated intervention. The Korean government attempted to create institutional environments where government, industry, and university could actively collaborate to develop indigenous technologies (Byon et al. 2002). The new mode of intervention greatly contributed to reducing uncertainties involved in the development of indigenous technologies (Hong 2006). The new model is similar to the previous model in the sense that it continued the past practices of "picking the winner" to promote the specific industrial sector, but the relationship has become reciprocal, in stark contrast to the hierarchical government-business relations during the high growth period.

The reciprocal relationship between government and business may signal the weakening of the state capacity (Kim 2008: 189). Rather it is reasonable to assume that changes in government role has an inverse relationship with the maturity of the industry. The government is likely to be dominant over the private sector in the initial stage as they should rely on government's policy support. By contrast, as the industry becomes mature, the government is likely to reduce the support to the industry and allocate resources to industries where the government support is more needed. Government-business relations can fluctuate, depending on the maturity of the industry rather than in a zero-sum situation for greater influence. This is a major reason why developmentalism and neoliberalism could coexist in the process of institutional transition in Korea. Although the Korean government began to embrace neoliberal policies, it did not abandon the developmentalist policies, particularly in promoting the targeted industries that are in the early stage of development.

The coexistence of developmentalism and neoliberalism does not allow the Korean government in the post-crisis period to intervene in the economy in the same way of the past. It is neither capable nor desirable for the government to replicate policies of the past, because shifting environments revealed the structural limitations of the developmental state. However, the Korean government still possesses transformative capacity to make active responses to rapidly changing international environments facilitated by globalization. As global value chains rapidly proliferated, the government should help domestic companies enter into upswing of the value chains in order to sustain economic growth (Evans 1995). The gist of this task lies in government ability to coordinate multiple players, given that competitive advantage depends on overall capacity of networks composed of multiple players rather than individual companies' capacity (Yeung 2016).[2] The government capacity of coordination was important even during the high growth period, but the Korean government selectively co-opted a few companies, or chaebols, as a partner for industrial targeting. In the post-crisis period, the Korean government attempted to form more encompassing and systematic networks of collaboration to coordinate diverse interests.

The Korean political economy evolves into the third model that incorporates elements of developmentalism and neoliberalism. While making transformation into a regulatory state, Korea still maintains developmentalist elements (Lee et al. 2002). Since the Asian financial crisis, the Kim Dae-jung government restrained itself in intervening in the economy to strengthen the market mechanism and strengthened regulations on big businesses to create fair and competitive market environments (Kim 2005). The dual nature of government policy is also found in labor as the Kim government simultaneously pursued labor flexibility and social safety (Kim 2008).

The Roh Moo-hyun government relied on indirect intervention by taking advantage of regulation as well. Recognizing that big businesses threaten fair competition, the Roh government tried to harness big businesses in an indirect manner by fortifying regulation. In reality, the Roh government drastically increased regulations on big businesses while continuously accepting their requests for deregulation. The Roh government introduced regulations limiting cross shareholding and cross payment guarantee that ultimately reinforced the government capacity. The Korean government could enhance its capacity by injecting massive public funds in the process of industrial restructuring. Although the Korean government implemented neoliberal policies in the post crisis period, the government approach is not fundamentally different from the traditional practices in that the government could improve its influence by controlling financial institutions (Lew and Wang 2007).

Developmentalist elements are also found in the Lee Myung-bak government, which is evaluated the most neoliberal, compared to other governments. While it pushed for neoliberal policies such as deregulation, liberalization, privatization, and tax reduction, the Lee government actively provided support to the private sector. The green growth strategy is a good case in point as the Lee government made efforts to create a virtuous circle between economic growth and environmental protection. In the wake of the global financial crisis in 2008, the Lee government also introduced a variety of complementary measures to financial liberalization, delaying the implementation of neoliberalism. The Lee government managed the speed and scope of financial liberalization that prompted its policy stance to derail from a

[2] Henry Yeung (2016) stresses "strategic coupling" among state, firm, and global production networks.

typical neoliberalism. In this sense, the Korea government in the post crisis period executed a combination of strategic reregulation and pro-competitive reregulation (Vogel 1996).

The neoliberal turn helped Korea not just overcome the Asian financial crisis, but also enter into the new stage of development by profoundly changing the primary nature of the Korean political economy. Due to the Asian financial crisis, Korea that had difficulty in shedding off the traditional developmentalism could fundamentally transform into a neoliberal (Pirie 2005). However, the existing studies tended to explore whether either developmentalism or neoliberalism constitutes a defining feature of the post crisis Korean political economy (Choi 2012; Kim 2008; Moon and Chung 2014; Park 2015).

For example, Kim argues that because Korea in the post crisis period embraced neoliberal programs while elements of developmentalism still remained in the path dependent way, the post-developmental state emerged where developmentalism and neoliberalism coexist (Kim 2013). While this observation is useful in pointing out that developmentalism and neoliberalism combined, it falls short of demonstrating how path dependence worked. Therefore, rather than weighing in the relative influence, we attempt to examine the way in which developmentalism and neoliberaliosm interact with each other to making a transition into a new model. We posit that developmentalism and neoliberalism make qualitative changes to produce self-reinforcing effects in the process of transition without leaning toward either of them. That is, the third type combining developmentalism and neoliberalism emerged in the post crisis period Korea.

Don Moon and Jinyoung Chung (2014) point out that it is important to identify dominant features rather than simply arguing that diverse features are mixed in the Korean political economy. In their view, neoliberal elements such as financial liberalization, market opening, deregulation, labor flexibility are the defining features of the Korean political economy. Although it is true that the Korean state's capacity temporarily increased in the process of crisis management, but because these changes were not institutionalized, the ultimate outcome was the transformation of the Korean model of development.

While it is reasonable to argue that it is crucial to identify the predominant characteristic of the Korean political economy, it is hasty to equate the emergence of neoliberal policies to the dissolution of developmentalism (Ha 2012). The Korean government did not implement neoliberal policies not just to promote market competition, but had mercantilist goals in mind because neoliberalism could serve as a means to help domestic companies compete against foreign companies. As long as the Korean government attempted to embrace neoliberal policies for developmentalist goals, the newly emerged Korean model of development neither converged to liberal market economy nor replicated traditional model of development.[3]

It is crucial to assess whether either developmentalism or neoliberalism has emerged as a dominant feature and/or developmentalism and neoliberalism

[3] At the same time, because the dynamics has unfolded unevenly across industrial sectors, one can find significant variations between industrial sectors (Lim 2010).

combined to create the third model. The majority of studies focus on the relative importance of the two paradigms (Pirie 2005), but we are interested in the way in which the two paradigms combine in the transition process, which is core characteristic of the newly emerged development model in Korea. Institutional transition takes place when interests of creating new institutions is greater than the costs of maintaining existing institutions (Vogel 2006). However, institutional rigidity delay or block institutional transition despite increasing costs of maintaining existing institutions.

1.4 Organization of the Book

In Chap. 2, we trace the political dynamics to explore the nature and mechanism of *chaebol* reform. For this, we focus on three cases: (1) lift of the ban on holding companies, (2) redesign of the regulation on *chaebol*'s investment, and (3) relaxation of the 4 percent rule. Although the Korean government attempted to carry out *chaebol* reform since the Asian financial crisis, views are divided on the primary nature of *chaebol*. The reason why the contradictory evaluations are made has to do with the fact that *chaebol* reform in Korea have taken diverse paths. The three cases demonstrate how the political dynamics of institutional change affected the divergence of *chaebol* reform, which depended on the interaction between interests and policy ideas. In the case of lifting the ban on holding companies, foreign investors and major players in Korea initially had different policy ideas. However, despite serious opposition from civil groups, the Kim Dae-jung government decided to legalize the holding company system as it perceived that the system is likely to improve Korean companies' competitiveness as well as facilitate corporate restructuring. The decision was made possible because the interests and policy ideas converged among the Kim Dae-jung government, foreign investors and international financial institutions, and *chaebol*.

In the case of regulation on *chaebol*'s investment, the limit on investment fluctuated depending on the political dynamics among the government, *chaebol*, and civil society. On the one hand, the pros of the investment limit argue that economic concentration exacerbated because chaebols could unduly diversify without any restrictions. On the other hand, the cons argue that it is anachronistic to impose investment limit that crippled *chaebols*' ability to compete in the age of globalization. Recognizing this subtle political balance, the political leadership had to maneuver to strengthen its political foundation and revitalize the economy, while siding with the general public's anti-chaebol sentiments. This political imperative essentially resulted in continuous fluctuation between regulation and deregulation on chaebols' investment limit.

The third case, deregulation of the 4 percent rule, shows political dynamics on the issue of whether industrial and financial capital should be separated. The separation of industrial and financial capital is an institutional foundation of the Korean developmental model during the high growth period. The Korean government selected chaebol as a main partner for industrialization, but did not allow chaebol to own or dominate banks because banks were an effective institutional means for the Korean government to control chaebol. However, bureaucrats in the finance ministry began to float the idea of deregulating the separation of industrial and financial capital under the Roh Moo-hyun government. And the Lee Myung-bak government became explicit to dismantle such regulation in the name of enhancing competitiveness of financial industry. The Lee government formed a strong policy coalition with *chaebol* to make substantial changes in the regulation, if not completely removed.

Chapter 3 examines the politics of privatization that was a driving force to dismantle the institutional foundation of the developmental state in Korea by looking into three cases: POSCO, KT, and Korea Development Bank (KDB). We posit that the privatization might have been inevitable under the dual pressures of globalization and democratization. However, the path and outcome of privatization varied because the process inevitably goes through dynamic interactions among stakeholders. Moreover, the politics of privatization is not managed by existing formal institutions, but by informal networks.

The three cases show different patterns of privatization in terms of how major stakeholders' incentive structures are constantly changing in the course of privatization, which was dominated by informal institutions. In the process of privatization, formal institutional changes such as outside directorship and the strengthening of protection for minority shareholders were made to increase transparency and accountability. Despite such institutional changes, however, informal institutions have a greater influence than formal institutions. Because not the substance but the form of South Korea's privatization and economic reform converged to global standards, it brought about a problem of mock-compliance. Informal networks made the privatized POSCO and KT degenerate into a target of government intervention. From this perspective, the three cases of privatization demonstrate that the developmental state in South Korea is not disappearing, but reappearing.

Chapter 4 explores the paradox of Korea, where legalization works as the institutional environment that causes informal networks to proliferate through the concept of the legalization trap. It particularly sheds light on how and why informal networks grew in Korea more rapidly and extensively despite the successful progress of the democratization and globalization. Since democratization and globalization, which progressed through the democratic transition in 1987 and the economic crisis in 1997, the discourse of transparency and accountability was widely discussed. Under the circumstance, a series of political economic reforms, institutional changes, and legislation did, in fact, strengthen the rule of law in Korea. But fundamental questions regarding transparency, responsibility, and formality were raised because informal networks are strengthened, although democratization and legalization proceeded in Korea. As a result, Korea suffers from "legalization trap."

In Chap. 5, we present the transformation of the IT industry as an example of the Korean government's adaptive capabilities in the face of rapidly changing internal and external environments. A stable policy network among major players was the backbone of the success of the Korean IT industry. While the Korean government took advantage of mounting external pressures from the US and the WTO to design the liberalization strategy, it also placed a high priority on recrafting the institutional arrangements where major stakeholders such as government ministries, universities, research institutes, and private companies could communicate and cooperate with other. In contrast to the traditional model of development, the Korean government focuses on the creation of a horizontal system where major stakeholders could cooperate on relatively equal terms.

However, it does not necessarily imply that major stakeholders did not have conflicts among them. There were many cases in which the government and private companies opposed to each other in envisioning the future path of technological development, as demonstrated in the case of CDMA vs. W-CDMA. Interestingly, despite the growing conflicts, major actors in the IT industry still preferred maintaining policy network, although dissenting views were growing between major players. This institutional dynamics stemmed from self-reinforcing mechanism. Despite growing conflicts, major players believed it could effectively alleviate strategic uncertainties, thereby taking a long term perspective in nurturing IT industry. Throughout this institutional dynamics, the Korean government, or the MIC, effectively managed uncertainties to harmonize the interests of private companies.

Chapter 6 explores the restructuring process of the aircraft industry since the Asian financial crisis. The case of the aircraft industry shows that since the Asian financial crisis the Korean government took an initiative in nurturing indigenous capabilities by restructuring of the aircraft industry, which was in deep trouble due to investment decline, cancellation of contracts, and increase in royalty payment. After the Korean government decided to create the KAI, it became an active supporter of industrial promotion particularly for the production of parts and components.

Since then, the Korean government and the KAI simultaneously sought to enhance indigenous capabilities as well as increase international collaboration. Although its ambitious plan to nurture autonomous capabilities ran into serious difficulty as demonstrated in the cases of indigenous development of the KFX, the Korean government skillfully launched T-50 program as an alternative. With its enhanced indigenous capabilities, the KAI also attempted to expand international collaboration to diversify its business portfolio. As a result, the KAI could increase its presence in the civilian sector as it strengthened its partnership with Boeing and Airbus.

The case of the aircraft industry demonstrates that the Korean government actively intervened in formulating new development strategies in order to simultaneously seek nurturing indigenous capabilities and increasing international collaboration. For this goal, the Korean government first took advantage of the Asian financial crisis to restructure the industry by merging major manufacturers to establish the KAI. The KAI with the help of the government embarked on the ambitious autonomous development plan. Under the situation the KAI had to discard the KFX program, the Korean government improvised the F-50 program to sustain the autonomous development capabilities. Recognizing that it is essential to improve its indigenous capabilities to increase international collaboration, the Korean government and the KAI played a central role in creating cooperative arrangements among existing producers so that they could stay in the business.

In Chap. 7, we explore the evolving nature of Korea's foreign economic policy, of which importance is increasingly bigger in shaping the Korean political economy. We first examine how and why the Korean government's interest in FTAs heightened in the late 1990s. We then move to explain the way in which Korea's FTA strategy transformed as the Korean government conceived FTAs' multifaceted nature. In particular, the Roh Moo-hyun government attempted to combine FTA policies and regional strategies. The Roh government recognized FTAs both as a means to consolidate institutionalized cooperation in East Asia as well as develop Korea into a regional and global FTA hub, edging over other East Asian countries. It is against this backdrop that the Korean government took the initiative in promoting FTA strategies instead of merely responding to the private sector's demand for trade liberalization.

Facing stronger opposition than initially anticipated, the Korean government attempted to shed light on the broad strategic nature of FTAs for the successful implementation of FTA strategies. Although the KORUS FTA would produce economic gains in general, support for it fluctuated. The Obama government's request for renegotiation of the KORUS FTA further exacerbated the general public's sentiment in Korea. Going through painful processes from negotiation to renegotiation and ratification of the KORUS FTA, the Korean government resorted to strategic implication of the KORUS FTA.

Despite the success, the Korean government's FTA strategy brought about unexpected consequences, because Korea was relatively retarded in making a policy shift to mega FTAs, in contrast to its previous policy shift to bilateral FTAs. Having observed strong opposition in the domestic arena in negotiating high quality FTAs such as the KORUS FTA, the Park Geun-hye government paid a greater attention to domestic compensation and streamlining of the policymaking structure rather than strategic implication of mega FTAs. The Park government's focus on reducing social costs associated with FTAs resulted in passive FTA strategies, departing from the previous governments' active FTA strategies.

References

Amsden, Alice. 1989. *Asia's Next Giant*. New York/Oxford: Oxford University Press.

Byon, Sang Kyu, Han Joo Kim, and Tae You Kim. 2002. Export-oriented Industrialization Strategy and Industrial Growth Factors in the 1990s: The Case of Mobile Phone Industry. *Journal of Information and Communications* 9 (2): 115–141. (in Korean).

Camdessus, Michael. 1999. "Crisis, Restructuring, and Recovery in Korea." Speech in Seoul. http://www.imf.org/external/np/speeches/1999/120299.htm. December.

Choi, Byung-Doo. 2012. Developmental Neoliberalism and the Hybridity of the Urban Policy of South Korea. In *Locating Neoliberalism in East Asia: Neoliberalizing Spaces in Developmental States*, ed. Bae-Gyoon Park, Richard Child Hill, and Asato Saito. Chichester: Blackwell Publishing.

Evans, Peter. 1995. *Embedded Autonomy: States and Industrial Transformation*. Princeton: Princeton University Press.

Ha, Yong Chool. 2012. Continuity and Change in the Institutional Foundations of Korean Crony Capitalism: A Preliminary Assessment. *Journal of Korean Politics* 21 (3): 207–248.

Hong, Sung Gul. 2006. The Political Economy of the IT Industry Development. In *Theory of New Growth State in the Information Age*, ed. Sung Gul Hong and Seok Man Yoon. Seoul: Nanam. (in Korean).

Hughes, Helen. 1999. Crony Capitalism and the East Asian Currency and Financial Crises. *Policy* 15: 3–9.

Ji, Joo-hyoung. 2009. The shift in the State form and mode of power exercise in South Korea: From the authoritarian developmental state to Neoliberal state power. *Korean Political Science Review* 43 (4): 175–203.

Kalinowski, Thomas. 2015. Crisis Management and the Diversity of Capitalism: Fiscal Stimulus Packages and the East Asian (neo-)Developmental State. *Economy and Society* 44 (2): 244–270.

Kang, David C. 2002. Bad Loans to Good Friends: Money Politics and the Developmental State in South Korea. *International Organization* 56 (1): 177–207.

Kim, Byung-kook, and Lim Hyuk-baek. 2000. The Myth and Reality of Crony Capitalism in East Asia. *Ideology Quarterly* 45: 7–74. (in Korean).

Kim, Young-In. 2013. From the Developmental State to the Post Developmental State: The Case of Lee Myung-bak Government's 'Low Carbon Green Growth' Policy. *The Korean Journal of Area Studies* 31 (1): 29–53. (in Korean).

Kim, Ihn Young. 2008. Revisting the Developmental State Theory in Korea: Changes in Developmental State and Its Characteristics since the 1997 Asian Financial Crisis. *Journal of Northeast Asian Studies* 47: 183–204. (in Korean).

Kim, Jeong Hae. 2005. Regulatory Reforms on Big Business and Changes in State's Role in Korea. *Korean Journal of Public Administration* 43 (4): 327–355. (in Korean).

Krugman, Paul. 1997. What ever happened to the Asian Miracle? Fortune. Aug. 18.

———. 1998. "The Capitalist; I Told You So." The New York Times Magazine. May 3.

Lee, Chung H., Keun Lee, and Kangkook Lee. 2002. Chaebol, Financial Liberalization, and Economic Crisis: Transformation of Quasi-Internal Organization in Korea. *Asian Economic Journal* 16: 17–35.

Lee, Seungjoo. 2004. Transforming the developmental state in Korea under Globalization. In *Handbook of development policy studies*, ed. Gedeon M. Mudacumura and M. Shamsul Haque, 509–522. New York: Marcel Dekker.

Lee, Seungjoo. 2018. The Asian financial crisis and the formation of the new political economy model in Korea. In *Political economic history of Korean model of developmental state*, ed. Hoon Jaung and Seungjoo Lee, 238–296. Seoul: Ingansarang. (in Korean).

Lee, Seungjoo, and Hyun Park. 2010. Self-Reinforcing Mechanism and Continuity in Policy Network: The Case of the IT Industry. *Journal of Korean Politics* 19 (3): 77–104. (in Korean).

Lew, Seok-Choon, and Hey Suk Wang. 2007. A Re-interpretation of Korean Economic Development through Social Capital: The Interplay of Strong State and Strong Society. *Society and Theory* 12: 109–162. (in Korean).

Lim, Haeran. 2008. Changes of industrial policy and governance in Korea. *Journal of Korean Politics* 17 (2): 1–32.

Lim, Haeran. 2010. The transformation of the developmental state and economic reform in Korea. *Journal of Contemporary Asia* 40 (2): 188–210.

MacIntyre, Andrew J., T.J. Pempel, and John Ravenhill, eds. 2008. *Crisis as Catalyst: Asia's Dynamic Political Economy*. Ithaca/London: Cornell University Press.

Mahoney, James. 2000. Path Dependence in Historical Sociology. *Theory and Society* 29 (4): 507–548.

Moon, Don, and Jin Young Chung. 2014. From 'Developmental State Model' to 'Neoliberal Model' – A Critical Assessment on the Debates of the 'Korean Developmental Model'. *Journal of Asia Pacific Studies* 21 (2): 129–164. (in Korean).

Park, Sang Young. 2015. Analysis on the Cohabitation of Developmentalism and Neoliberalism in Korea: Changes in the Korean Developmental State since the 1990s and Varieties of Developmental-Neoliberal Mixes. *Journal of Asia Pacific Studies* 22 (4): 5–40. (in Korean).
Pierson, Paul. 1999. Increasing Returns, Path Dependence, and the Study of Politics. *American Political Science Review* 94 (2): 251–267.
Pirie, Iain. 2005. The new Korean State. *New Political Economy 10*(1): 25–42.
Rhyu, Sang-Young, and Seungjoo Lee. 2006. Economic Reform and Changes in Informal Networks between Government and Business in South Korea. *Journal of 21st Century Political Science* 16 (1): 43–66. (in Korean).
Shin, Jang-Sup, and Ha-Joon Chang. 2003. *Restructuring Korea Inc*. London: RoutledgeCourzon.
Stubbs, Richard. 2009. What ever happened to the East Asian Developmental State? The Unfolding Debate. *The Pacific Review* 22 (1): 1–22.
Thurbon, Elizabeth. 2001. "Two paths to financial liberalization: South Korea and Taiwan." *The Pacific Review* 14 (2): 241–267.
Um, Kyusook, Hyun-Chin Lim, and Suk-Man Hwang. 2014. South Korea's developmental state at a crossroads: Disintegration or re-emergence 45(2): 211–253.
Vogel, Steven K. 2006. *Japan Remodeled: How Government and Industry Are Reforming Japanese Capitalism*. Ithaca: Cornell University Press.
Vogel, Steven. 1996. *Freer Markets, More Rules: Regulatory Reform in Advanced Industrial Countries*. Ithaca: Cornell University Press.
Wade, Robert. 1990. *Governing the market: Economic theory and role of government in East Asian industrialization*. Princeton: Princeton University Press.
Wade, Robert, and Frank Veneroso. 1998. The Asian Crisis: The High Debt Model versus the Wall Street-Treasury-IMF Complex. *New Left Review* 228: 3–20.
Weiss, Linda. 2000. Developmental States in Transition: Adapting, Dismantling, Innovating, not 'Normalizing'. *The Pacific Review* 13 (1): 21–55.
Woo-Cumings, Meredith. 1999. *The Developmental State*. Ithaca: Cornell University Press.
Yang, Jae Jin. 2005. Developmentalism after Development: Growth, Crisis, and Future of the Korean Developmental State. *Korean Public Administration Review* 39 (1): 1–18. (in Korean).
Yeung, Henry Wei-chung. 2016. *Strategic Coupling: East Asian Industrial Transformation in the New Global Economy*. Ithaca: Cornell University Press.
Yoon, Sang Woo. 2009. Internalizing Neoliberal Globalization in Korea: A Case for 'Developmental Neoliberalization'. *Economy and Society* 83: 40–68. (in Korean).

Chapter 2
Policy Ideas and Interest Alignment in the Process of Institutional Change in Chaebol Reform

2.1 Why Has Chaebol Reform Undergone Diverse Paths?

Reform is multi-faceted. Looking back on the history of South Korea's political economy, South Korean society has displayed diverse patterns of economic reform in terms of goals, contents, means, and processes. Winners and losers have different notions of reform based on what potential benefit they can get from institutional change. Different stakeholders and actors may assume and pursue different goals, interests, ideas, and patterns of reform throughout the whole process of institutional change. Only fact we can agree on is that all reforms, for better or worse, take the form of institutional change. How can we identify the mechanism or politics, which often remain vague and mysterious, of institutional change? To answer these puzzles, we need to elaborate on institutional analysis by tracing the detailed process and examining how related variables interact on a specific issue in a critical period. Decoding the mechanism of institutional change has been one of the main research tasks in neo-institutional political economy. Diverse paths of institutional change can reflects the nature of real politics that define the internal workings of state behavior.

After the 1997 Asian financial crisis, the reform of South Korea's *chaebol* drew considerable attention from both academic and practical worlds. Questions such as the following have been raised: Have South Korea's *chaebol* changed? If the *chaebol* have changed, what changed and who triggered and led the change? If there was no change, why have they not changed and what is impeding the change? What is the unique aspect of the process and characteristics in the institutional change shown in the reform process of South Korea's *chaebol*? This chapter seeks to explore the paths and driving forces of change in three cases of economic institutions, which have been the major debates for *chaebol* reform in Korea since the Asian financial crisis in 1997. Three issues portray the divergent paths of institutional change and *chaebol* reform in Korea along with the political dynamics of institutional change: (1) how to lift the ban

S. Lee and S. Rhyu, *The Political Economy of Change and Continuity in Korea*,
The Political Economy of the Asia Pacific, https://doi.org/10.1007/978-3-319-71453-0_2

on holding companies, (2) how to redesign the regulation on the gross amount of investment allowed in major big business groups, and (3) how to deregulate the 4 percent rule to protect financial capital from being merged with industrial capital.

While the three issues form the core of the South Korean government's competition policy, they have been contentious in discussing *chaebol* reform. There were conflicts between the pro and cons regarding all aspects of institutional change, including the speed, scope, method, principal agent, and direction. Institutional change always creates winners and losers. The entire process of institutional change explicitly reflected the complex politics that occur as players struggle to win and avoid becoming losers. However, it is not easy to accurately draw the complicated politics of institutional change into one analytical framework. Despite many existing institutional analyses, there remain numerous issues that is hardly explained by conventional wisdom.

We emphasize several factors frequently used in institutional analysis to disclose more clearly and closely the reasons of institutional change. First, this paper analyzes the process and mechanism of institutional change rather than institutional change itself. This research is premised on the idea that the process of institutional change determines the outcome. Second, the concepts of interest and policy idea, which are used as conflicting variables in rational choice institutionalism and organizational institutionalism respectively, are emphasized as the core independent variables of institutional change. It also highlights the idea that the pattern and route of institutional change may shift according to the interaction between interest and policy ideas. Third, regarding the influence external pressure has on domestic institutional change, this chapter focuses on interest alignment between domestic actors instead of discussing the degree of external pressure.

The chapter is organized in the following way. The second part critically reviews existing institutionalist theories to construct the conceptual framework. The three cases analyzed in this chapter are unique because they underwent changes and reversals in a short period of time. Part three emphasizes gaps in policy ideas between foreign investors and domestic policy decision makers concerning issues related to lifting the ban on holding companies. The historical memory regarding holding companies and the gap between policy ideas determined the pattern of institutional change that relaxed regulations toward holding companies. Part four analyzes the process of alleviating and strengthening the ceiling on the gross amount of investment allowed. This case is an example where the direction and pattern of institutional change were determined by the change of the interest structure and incentives between domestic coalitions to strengthen and relax regulations in a relatively short period of time, irrelevant to pressure from foreign capital or interests. Part five analyzes the Lee Myung-bak administration's sudden attenuation process of regulation preventing the fusion of industrial capital and financial capital. In this case, each actor's individual interests are important variables. In particular, it is revealed that sudden institutional change is possible when the interests and policy ideas of the president and *chaebol* align. Part six presents the theoretical implications found in the case analyses to conclude the paper.

2.2 The Politics of Institutional Change: Policy Ideas, Interest Alignments, and the Role of External Pressure

Institutionalism emphasizes institutions as the most essential independent variable in analyzing human behavior, economic growth, societal change, and sources of power. Types of institutionalism are categorized in line with how the concept and role of institutions are defined and how the process of the building and change of institutions is analyzed. Types of institutionalism include rational choice institutionalism, historical institutionalism, organizational institutionalism, sociological institutionalism, and discursive institutionalism (Schmidt 2008). These paradigms started in earnest as an attempt to overcome the methodological limitations of the traditional structural-functionalist approach that was popular in the 1960s and 1970s. The intellectual origin of institutionalism traces back to the nineteenth century, when scholars began to philosophically agonize over the root of human society along with development of capitalism. Many philosophers such as Max Weber and Karl Marx started to research politics, the nation, power, economy, the market, and society using an interdisciplinary method. Most core concepts and logic recently receiving attention in institutionalism are problems that have been deeply ruminated over by a few key scholars for a long period of time. Especially from the 1990s, new institutionalism has been more actively discussed and developed for the purpose of refuting and supplementing neo-classicalism, the developmental state, and cultural approaches.

Regardless of the types of other paradigms within institutionalism, some notions and arguments that most literature in new institutionalism commonly agree on are useful in explaining reform and the process of institutional change of South Korean *chaebol*. First of all, institutions both restrict human behavior and social phenomena, and also facilitate change. Institutions, on the one hand, tend to constrain and shape the range of options from which actors are likely to choose as they engage in the political process of institutional change. However, on the other hand, institutions also provide principles, practices, and opportunities that actors use assertively as they pursue their interests and goals (Campbell 2004, 8). While historical institutionalism and organizational institutionalism emphasize the constraints of institutions and recognize that institutional change is both incremental and path-dependent, rational choice institutionalism signifies rational choice based on economic interests pursued by individuals even within constraints.

South Korea's *chaebol* had to participate in economic activities under institutional constraints created by the state, such as regulations and competition policy. However, *chaebol* repeatedly grew by continuously attempting to alleviate institutional constraints for the strategic interests of their companies, or by using the existing institutions as a justification to expand. Secondly, institutions are composed of formal and informal institutions. Formal institutions refer to laws, acts, agreements, and procedures, and informal institutions indicate norms, customs, beliefs, codes of behavior, rules, networks, and culture and traditions within a community (North 1990, 4). Institutionalism, including rational choice institutionalism and historical institutionalism, perceives human behavior to be structured by a combination of formal institutions and informal rules. In organizational institutionalism, discursive institutionalism, and sociological institutionalism, informal rules such as taken-for-granted cultural frameworks, scripts, cognitive schema, historical traditions, and cultural inertia are emphasized as dominant variables (Schmidt 2012). Policy ideas or self-interest, major variables in this chapter, may be the rationally chosen outcome of actors or agents from the perspective of rational choice institutionalism. But from the perspective of organizational and sociological institutionalism, they can be seen as products naturally created in compliance with informal institutions that have already been long embedded in a particular society.

In South Korea's political economy, institutional change can be easy or interrupted, depending on how formal institutions and informal institutions are combined. In particular, the issue of mock-compliance, which is criticized in South Korea's *chaebol* reforms, is a concept which shows that informal rules and networks can play a more important role (Guillen 2003; Leković 2011, 363–367). No matter how well formal institutions are designed to modernize corporate governance, if informal rules or culture, which are difficult for formal institutions to influence, are not reformed, then it is difficult for South Korean corporate governance to comply with global standards. The core challenge of South Korean economic reform is how to reduce the gap between formal institutions and informal rules.

Third, formal institutions can change easily, but informal institutions do not change overnight. For formal institutions, when a new law is enacted or revised, existing institutions disappear or new institutions are built. New institutions among countries are formed through international agreements such as FTAs. Complicated politics certainly apply in the change process of formal institutions, so diverse patterns of institutional change appear by country and by case. But the change is made in a relatively short period of time compared to changes in informal rules. Although the corporate governance structure of stock companies is the most classic target and result of international regulation, even in the case of Netherlands, the birthplace of the system, there remain unusual informal institutions. This is because informal institutions or cultural characteristics, which are embedded in political settings and social structures, still strongly define institutional change and corporate governance structures. In Japanese corporate governance structure reform, there is a stronger resistance against foreign investors in a sector with stronger embeddedness, so in such a case, compliance with global standards is the lowest (Ahmadjian and Robbins 2005). In South Korea's *chaebol* reforms, it is not an exaggeration to say that the changes that occurred in informal rules determine the outcome of the whole institutional change.

Fourth, it cannot be denied that policy ideas emphasized in historical institutionalism, or the notion of interest emphasized in rational choice institutionalism, are important factors in explaining individual behavior or the operation principle of society. Yet, a more important question is *whose* ideas and *whose* interests they are. No matter how advanced a country's democracy is, its political economic power and resources are unevenly distributed. Universal suffrage or expanded enfranchisement cannot represent the power relations in the actual market and politics. So, it is important to see what ideas and what interests a person or a group in an important position in a power structure has. Institutional arrangements reflect power relations. It is difficult to find a case that equally fulfills everyone's ideas and interests in the process of institutional change. The same political change can be positive reform for some people, and change for the worse for others. In reality, it is difficult for the general purpose and outcome of reform to be universally accepted by all groups. In the discussion of East Asian regionalism, the same understanding can be applied to the analysis that the idea that each major East Asian leader has regarding regionalism and globalization determines the outcome towards regionalism (Acharya 2009). At least in South Korea, the ideas and interests of laborers or farmers are not that meaningfully reflected in the formation of various regional institutions such as FTAs.

Fifth, when investigating the questions of who builds institutions and when, it is generally agreed that normally institutions shape politics, and in a crisis politics shape institutions. In Douglas North's book, he raises the question of "Are we free because we have a constitution, or do we have constitution because we are free?" (North 1990). He argues that during a time of peace, humans can be free because of laws and institutions, and during a crisis humans can create new laws and institutions due to political choice. In other words, "institutions explain everything until they explain nothing" (North 1990). In a society like South Korea, where many political economic incidents and institutional changes were compressed into a short period of time, the politics of actors who build and change new institutions explain more than the constraints provided by institutions. In particular, to analyze the drastic changes and reforms at major critical junctures such as the Korean War in 1950, the 1961 military coup, the 1987 democratic consolidation, the 1997 Asian Financial Crisis, and the 2008 Global Financial Crisis, we should look at the role of politics in punctuated equilibrium or institutional discontinuity rather than institutional continuity (Moon and Rhyu 2010).

Even if we accept the usefulness of institutionalism, methodological challenges to explain the various patterns of institutional change and political dynamics still remain. First of all, there are many discussions regarding institutional change, but most analyses concentrate on the causes, agents, and triggers of institutional change. The major factors of these analyses are the intensity, strategic interest relations of domestic interest groups, and the ideas and leadership style of the chief policy decision makers, and the majority of the key issues are contracted as competition and the interaction of globalization versus the nation-state (Cortell and Peterson 2002; Lee 2005, 2008; Gourevitch and Shinn 2005; Lim 2010). However, there is a frustration in empirically describing the specific mechanism of the process of institutional change. In actuality, there are innumerable factors that trigger institutional change. It is difficult to concretely specify, detect, locate, and trace what interests and purpose each actor has towards institutional change, and explain how they drive institutional change. Moreover, it is difficult to fully reveal the interactions or correlation of all actors.

Second, much research on institutionalism focuses on comparing or categorizing the pattern of institutional change by analyzing the degree and scope of institutional change. In other words, the research categorizes whether institutional change is incremental, or evolutionary, or whether it is episodic, or revolutionary. Even in the same case of institutional change, depending on the time frame, it can be analyzed as being incremental or revolutionary. An incremental change can be seen as a revolutionary one if one analyzes a brief period. On the contrary, a revolutionary change can be categorized as an incremental one when a long period is analyzed. According to the time frame, a microscopic change can create a great discontinuity, and a large macroscopic change can merely be an incremental continuity. Cases of institutional change, including the enactment of the 1890 Sherman Act and the 1914 Clayton Act, changes in economic philosophy after the Great Depression, changes in world order after the end of the Cold War in 1991, and the adoption of the 2014 PPACA: Patient Protection and Affordable Care Act also known as Obamacare, can all be identified differently depending on the time frame used in analysis.

Third, there are many core concepts that are used in institutional analysis that are not yet clearly defined, or which remain controversial according to contending paradigms. The notion of policy idea, which appears as an important independent variable in the process of institutional change, is also largely vague and controversial (Campbell 2004, 91–92). Ideas may include policy, norms, beliefs, programs, and philosophy, and appear in different forms, such as narratives, frames, frames of reference, discursive fields of ideas, argumentative practices, storytelling, and collective memories. The policy ideas provide guidelines for political action and serve to justify programs through arguments focused on their interest-based logic and necessity (Hall 1989; Schmidt 2010, 2). The policy ideas may also change when windows of opportunity open in the face of events, and as old policies no longer solve the problems or fit the politics for which they were designed (Kingdon 1984; Seabrooke 2006). These changes may be fast or slow, and they may be incremental or abrupt. But what remains unclear is whether events drive change in policy ideas or whether ideas open windows, creating new opportunities for policy change, and what makes actors believe that windows of opportunity are open (Campbell 2004; Schmidt 2010).

How and on what level, and under what sequence, do policy ideas and interests influence each other? In rational choice institutionalism, interest is the most important factor of institutional change (North 1990). When an existing institution does not benefit the actor, and becomes less efficient, political action towards institutional change begins. On the other hand, in historical institutionalism or organizational institutionalism, political ideas and interests are already reflected in the institution and organization, so interests do not trigger institutional change, and action and interests are constrained by rules, procedures, norms, and cultural frames (Steinmo et al. 1992). However, confusion regarding the conceptual category of ideas and interests still remains. Currently, there is no agreed upon point of view stating whether policy ideas cover interests or whether interests incorporate policy ideas, or if it is meaningless to differentiate between interests and policy ideas in the actual stage of change of an institution. Furthermore, there is no consensus regarding whether it is ideas or interests that are first defined. On the one hand, policy ideas may come before interests, acting as ‘road maps’ for individual actors to clarify their goals or limit the range of strategies to be taken – in which case ideas seem to determine interests. However, if this is the case, then we still have no explanation of the selection mechanism by which certain ideas get chosen over others. On the other hand, ideas may come after interests, acting as 'focal points' for actors to choose among equally acceptable alternatives – in which case ideas serve at best to 'mop up' residual variance, and we still can't explain the mechanism by which the now exogenously interest-determined ideas are picked. In addition, interests and ideas are not fixed, and can shift according to various elements in each phase. So the relation and interaction between interests and ideology becomes more complicated.

Then, how can we identify the unique pattern of institutional change in South Korea's *chaebol* reform? South Korean institutional change, particularly the series of *chaebol* reforms that progressed after the 1997 Asian Crisis, was fast in speed and broad in scope, the pattern was very abrupt and drastic, and external pressure and the state are seen to have played the biggest role. This sort of change can be compared to Japan's slow and incremental change and the development of China's private sector (ten Brink 2011; Nee and Opper 2012), and also to the market or society-led pattern of reform in the US or Europe's. However, looking at specific cases, it is difficult to identify institutional change in a single pattern, and there are various elements that trigger institutional change. In addition, according to the time period, there are plenty of phenomena that make it difficult to see that South Korea's institutional reform was fast and abrupt. In reality, after almost 20 years of a series of economic reforms that were instituted following the 1997 Asian Crisis, there is wide acceptance of the criticism that South Korea's *chaebol* did not in fact change. Recently, there is a phenomenon that the developmental state, which was a target of reform, is not dissolving, but is rather reviving and reorganizing. Within the argument that regardless of numerous changes in formal institutions, many informal networks and culture deeply embedded in South Korean society and politics have not changed (Lee and Rhyu 2008), there are also arguments suggesting that as a source of external pressure, foreign investors do not always pursue transparency and accountability, but sometimes hinder and delay reform for their own interests.

Meanwhile, in many cases of institutional change, there has been a frequent reshuffling of structure and power relations of pro-reform and anti-reform coalitions concerning *chaebol* reform. Then, efforts to identify South Korea's institutional change pattern into a single model and to compare it with the patterns of other countries may no longer be valid. A more academically meaningful research task may be undertaking a detailed case analysis to reveal that there are diverse patterns and paths of institutional change.

This chapter attempts to answer the questions of why and how does South Korea's institutional change shows a variety of patterns and routes. First of all, it focuses on the process and mechanism of institutional change. Institutionalists claim that institutions enable, empower, facilitate, constitute, and constrain actors, by which institutions help to guide or shape action. However, institutions do not work in vacuum. Institutions and actors constantly interact with and influence each other. Then, what make institutions work? How do institutions work better or worse? How do institutions and actors interact? How can we describe and identify the detailed inner mechanisms and process of institutional change?

This chapter conducts case studies to suggest a more detailed answer to these questions. It analyzes the cases of the relaxation of regulations regarding the establishment of or transfer into holding companies, the change of restraints on the gross amount of investment within *chaebol* groups, and the change in 4 percent regulation to prevent the fusion of financial and industrial capital. The scope, purpose, and issues of institutional change are clear in each case, and they took place within a relatively short period of time. However, the interests and ideas of many actors were bound up intensely with one another. How such ideas and interests have changed, along with how they are tied to action, will be traced using the concept of "process tracing" (Campbell 2004, 121). On a micro-level, this chapter analyzes how policy coalitions are reshuffled around the objective, scope, and path of institutional change.

Second, this chapter emphasizes the combination form of policy ideas and interests as the independent variable that determines the unique pattern and route of institutional change. How policy ideas and the interests of major actors combine, and how the combined form reshuffles during the process of institutional change, determines the pattern and path of institutional change. The nature of the process or mechanism of institutional change, which this paper aims to emphasize, can become more precise by analyzing how policy ideas and interests interact. These ideas serve as guides and principles to actors on what to do, as well as the source of justification and legitimation.

Actors pursue their interests by identifying and promoting their personal interests as the substance of ruling ideas and discourse (Campbell 2004, 28). However, interests are subjective ideas, which, though real, are neither objective nor material. On top of that, ideas and interests are dynamic, intersubjective constructs rather than static structures. They evolve over time and change their real face along with controversial policy issues. Moreover, the ideas and interests of actors sometimes diverge rather than converge over specific timing or issues. This paper carefully specifies detailed behavior, remarks, and stories on how the major actors in each case reflect their ideas and interests. It also specifically reconstructs the dynamic politics within an appropriate time frame over how interest-based policy coalitions disaggregate or reorganize.

Lastly, this chapter analyzes whether the interests of foreign actors, which are the source and substance of external pressure, are aligned with the interests of domestic actors as an independent variable rather than analyzing the existence or degree of external pressure. If their interests are aligned, the width of institutional change broadens, its pace quickens, and the direction tends to become irreversible. However, when their interests collide and the direction of reform diverges, institutional change is restricted and delayed, and according to the change in political economic conditions, the path of institutional change becomes a zigzag form.

While it is true that the pressure of globalization is pushing for domestic institutional reform, the interest of foreign investors is to make money, not to positively reform the institutions of host countries. Transparency and accountability do not necessarily guarantee the interests of foreign investors. Furthermore, the composition and interests of foreign investors are not monolithic. They vary according to industry, country of origin, and by reform issue. We cannot simply assume that the interests of foreign investors will always be coherent and unified on specific issues. Although the strong pressure of globalization cannot be ignored, no matter how weak the host country is, the domestic politics of a nation-state still remain an important factor that determines the path of institutional change. No matter how strong external pressure is, there is no case that does not pass through the state mediation of the host country and that reforms or changes institutions exactly according to the demands of external pressure. Consequently, to realize their interests, foreign investors search for a policy coalition partner within the host country who shares their ideas and interests. The existing institutionalism perspective which provides an opposing analysis that dichotomizes globalization and the nation-state cannot capture this interest alignment mechanism. These three cases concretely portray the various politics of interest alignment between foreign investors and domestic actors.

2.3 Lifting the Ban on Holding Companies: The Conflict of Ideas Between the Government and Foreign Investors

2.3.1 Divergent Ideas Between the State and Foreign Investors

A holding company is a parent corporation that owns outstanding voting stock in another company. It does not produce goods and services itself and exists only to hold shares of and to control affiliated companies. It generally controls the board of directors of son or grandson corporations using the power of ownership or invested capital, thereby deciding and monitoring their key policies and management. The benefits of using a holding company can be numerous and span everything from stronger creditor protection and tax savings to making a business more saleable through easier acquisition and divestiture planning. On the flip side, the disadvantages of having a holding company are for the most part limited to the added legal and accounting costs and complexity associated with incorporating and maintaining one. These key benefits, for investors, which are not typically available through regular corporate structure, outweigh the cost of changing an existing regular company to a holding company or of founding a new holding company. Many large corporations in modern capitalist markets, such as General Electric or Bank of America, take the form of a holding company.

Even though the forms of holding companies may be identical, the policy ideas surrounding them can be extremely different. The social norms, historical traditions and memories, and policy frames surrounding a holding company can be formed not just around the management and organizational advantages and convenience, but also from the unique political economic characteristics shown in a particular society's history of capitalism and growth process of the company. In the history of Anglo-Saxon capitalism, holding companies are one of the most modernized forms of corporations to develop in capitalism by protecting the investors and expanding investment. As Anglo-Saxon countries experienced the damage of the monopoly of large conglomerates as early as the nineteenth century, and created strong anti-trust laws and monitoring systems to regulate this monopoly power, there was the simultaneous creation of a social norm to monitor and minimize the harmful effects of holding companies. There was a strong positive policy idea towards holding companies. For foreign investors, holding companies were the strongest institutions that embody the keywords of globalization, transparency, and accountability. After the 1997 Asian financial crisis, foreign investors and international financial organizations such as the IMF and the World Bank strongly pushed the South Korean government to allow holding companies in order to achieve South Korean *chaebol* reform.

In South Korea's history of capitalism, holding companies were a type of corporation that held extremely negative images and memories. First of all, in South Korean society, holding companies immediately brings up the image of the old Japanese large conglomerates before the Second World War. The South Korean government fostered *chaebol*, which copied the form of the Japanese *zaibatsu*, as the champions of economic growth. Japanese *zaibatsu*, combined with Japanese militarism, were perceived as having colonized South Korea, supporting imperialism during the World War II and committing numerous war crimes. They were symbols of opacity, collusion, recession cartels, market monopoly, the forced drafting and exploitation of South Koreans, and the destruction of democracy.

This impression and historical memory of old Japanese *zaibatsu* were not limited to South Korea. The first measure taken as part of 'post-war democratic reform', which the MacArthur general headquarters (GHQ) implemented in 1946 after their occupation of Japan, dismantled six holding companies of large conglomerates in the finance and industry sectors, and introduced a system prohibiting the establishment of pure holding companies. The GHQ perceived holding companies of large conglomerates as the economic foundation that started the war, monopolized the market, and destroyed democracy. With the start of the Cold War in 1947, MacArthur allowed for the establishment of operating holding companies in Japan in alignment with the changing strategic interests of the US. However, the international society continues to hold a negative policy idea towards Japanese *zaibatsu*. Until 1997, pure holding companies were not allowed in Japan.

In addition, the 1997 economic crisis was sufficient to maximize South Korean society's negative perception of holding companies. At the time, there was a strong belief among South Koreans that the cause of the economic crisis lay in the typical management failure of *chaebol*, such as reckless diversification strategies, sloppy management, family-controlled management, corrupt links between business and politics, and excessive loan management. The dominant perception was that *chaebol* who had received active support from the Park Chung-hee administration rather indulged themselves in opaque management practices and corruption, and their absorption of the too-big-to-fail practice brought on the economic crisis and pain to the people. As the old *zaibatsu* holding companies of Japan had left behind the pains of war, South Korea's *chaebol* now brought the 'sovereign default' crisis to South Korea.

It strengthened the negative image of and critical policy ideas toward holding companies. In this situation, it was unimaginable to allow South Korea's *chaebol* to establish holding companies. Furthermore, after 1986 in South Korea, various *chaebol* regulation policies were strengthened through the Monopoly Regulation and Fair Trade Act with the objective of constraining the economic concentration of the top 30 corporate groups. These restrictions included ceilings on the gross amount of investment, prohibition of the establishment of or transfer to holding companies, prohibition of mutual investment, restrictions on debt guarantees, and prohibition of the fusion of financial capital with industrial capital.

It became clear that there was a large gap between foreign investors and major players in Korea in terms of policy ideas towards holding companies. The legalization of holding companies was a good direction of reform for foreign investors but it was a change for the worse for the general public in Korea. Such a gap in policy ideas was a factor that made the institutional change legalizing holding companies, which was proposed as the core tool of *chaebol* reform by foreign investors and international financial institutions right after the 1997 economic crisis, difficult. From the perspective of foreign investors at the time, it was a rational method to improve the transparency and accountability of the *chaebol*. Although they strongly pressured the South Korean government, the Kim Dae-jung administration resisted the demand to allow the establishment of holding companies even as he actively accepted all other demands.

2.3.2 Converging Interests Among Stakeholders

Regardless of this undeniable existence of gap in policy ideas, what was the main factor that made the South Korean government change its initial opinion opposing the legalization of holding companies and suddenly agree to do so? The background behind South Korea's initial opposition and subsequent turnaround 15 months later seems to lie in the convergence of interests between the related domestic economic stakeholders and those applying external pressure. Following the demand by the Federation of Korean Industries (FKI) to permit the transformation of holding companies on February 4th, 1998 the Fair Trade Commission (FTC) restrictively allowed for *chaebol* to transform into holding companies in May of 1999 only after going through a complicated review process. The FTC announced a legislative bill allowing only corporations that had completely settled their mutual debt guarantees between *chaebol* corporations to transform into holding companies.

The Asian financial crisis facilitated rapid changes in corporate governance structure. An economic environment with a completely open capital market and legalized hostile takeovers has made increasing competitiveness and protecting management rights an urgent challenge for South Korea's *chaebol*. Even before the economic crisis, *chaebol* demanded that holding companies be legalized. As a countermeasure to this market pressure, on February 4th, 1998, the FKI formally suggested that the government permit the establishment of holding companies for the first time (*Chosun Ilbo*, February 5, 1998a).[1] It was the business world's response to the measure passed by then president-elect Kim Dae-jung's emergency planning committee, which allowed hostile takeovers. The FKI argued that "efficiency in corporate governance structure should be sought by permitting the establishment of holding companies, and the capability of management rights to engage in defense should be ensured through the creation of holding companies." Following this request, the FKI made several more proposals to permit the early establishment of pure holding companies in its meetings with related departments, (*The Korea Economic Daily*, April 9, 1998a). The FKI's demand was affected by the demands of foreign capital that hoped to invest in South Korea. The UK semiconductor communications company GEC group and the engineering company TI group conveyed to the South Korean government through various channels the point that even with investment, without the ability to establish holding companies, there would be difficulty in financial management (*Dong-A Ilbo*, December 16, 1998). Similar to Japan's lift of its ban on holding companies, the demands of foreign corporations to invest directly influenced the decision to lift the ban on holding companies.

There was strong external pressure demanding South Korea to lift its ban on holding companies. Along with realistic demands that lifting the ban on holding companies was needed, there was also a strong perception that transparent business management and *chaebol* reform were required. When the IMF approved the fund withdrawal of the scheduled two billion dollars on February 17th 1998, it proposed conditions to improve the transparency of corporate governance structure in South Korea, including the obligation to combine financial statements and improve accountability to stockholders. Through the abolishment of mandatory bids, domestic hostile takeovers were agreed to (Ministry of Finance and Economy, IMF Measures Task Force, February 1998). At the second meeting for the introduction of structural adjustment loans on September 25, 1998, the World Bank applied direct and active pressure, declaring that it would not provide the two billion dollars if South Korea did not "revise the Monopoly Regulation and Fair Trade Act permitting holding companies and preventing economic concentration" (Ministry of Finance and Economy, Public Loans Task Force, September 1998; *Joongang Ilbo*, September 25, 1998a).[2]

Domestic politics in the US and the lobby of related industries also acted as external pressure on South Korea for *chaebol* reforms, including pressure to lift the ban on holding companies. At the federation budget review that included the additional supply of 18 billion dollars to the IMF, US Congress specified a special regulation measure so that IMF funds would not support certain parts of businesses in South Korea (The United States Senate, October 2, 1998, Title 6 Sec. 602). In other

[1]At the time, management rights were seriously threatened due to a decline of corporate value of over 50% compared to the end of 1996 as a result of the reduction of stock prices and the exchange rate (*The Chosun Ilbo*, February 5, 1998a).

[2]The agreement was delayed for 4 months due to the World Bank's conditions for providing structural adjustment loans of two billion dollars. As the government agreed to accept most of the demands, they reached an agreement on September 24, 1998.

words, it prohibited government subsidies, tax privileges, and relief loans towards corporations and industries related to semiconductors, steel, automobile, shipbuilding, textiles, and clothing. There was also an obligation for the US Minister of Finance to regularly report to the Congress to check compliance (*Dong-A Ilbo*, December 16, 1998).[3]

Compared to the US side, South Korean business' demand for the lifting of the ban was relatively modest. The FKI emphasized abolishment of regulations that could introduce corporate governance such as the prohibition of the establishment of holding companies, suggested by the OECD's recommendation of corporate governance structure reform guidelines (The Federation of Korean Industries, November 1998, 2). Although the FKI demanded that the government lift the ban on holding companies as a precondition to *chaebol* reform, it did not make specific suggestions. While holding companies were a possible alternative for the business circle, a sudden change to a holding company system was impossible in reality. Samsung group's 1998 management renovation plan was the first formalized reference to holding companies at the individual corporate group level (Samsung Office of the Secretary, January 1998, 10).[4]

After a short period of time, the Kim Dae-jung administration was in a situation where the legalization of holding companies would earn political gains due to the strong external pressure and changes in domestic political economy. The government was aware that the holding companies system should be introduced to strengthen competitiveness and promote corporate restructuring. The economic reform proposal[5] reported by the then president-elect Kim Dae-jung's economic policy task force, or the emergency economic measures committee, included lifting the ban on holding companies.

However, the Kim Dae-jung government faced opposition even from government agencies. On November 18, 1997, the FTC opposed the business circle's demands to lift the ban on holding companies, stating that it was premature to establish holding companies (*Joongang Ilbo*, November 18, 1997b). Chun Yoon-chul, the chairman of the FTC, affirmed that "at the moment, our conditions do not yet allow for the autonomous correction of the harmful effects of economic concentration" and implied that it would maintain its regulations that permit economic concentration (Chun 1997, 2). Caught between external pressure from international financial institutions and domestic opposition, the Kim Dae-jung administration decided on a position that would restrictively lift the ban on holding companies with the presumption that

[3] In a letter the US Secretary of the Treasury sent to Congress, the evaluation results stated that the IMF funds were not used to financially support these six industries, and it was reported that the debt of these sectors was not guaranteed.

[4] Even here, the transformation to holding companies is not mentioned, but there is an indirect expression of opinion stating that "if holding companies are legally permitted" that it would reform the organization accordingly.

[5] In the government report "100 Policy Tasks to be promoted by the New Government," the "policy to allow holding companies during the president's term in office, and to abolish the ceiling on the gross amount of investment according to the complete permission of hostile takeovers" was specified.

it would minimize the harmful effects of economic concentration. On January 19th 1998, Chun Yoon-chul determined that "with introduction of consolidated financial statements, the establishment of holding companies will be permitted," showing a leap of change in policy (*Maeil Business News*, January 20, 1998a).

A complicated political process was developed centering around the interest relations regarding the conditions of lifting the ban on holding companies. Influenced by Japan having lifted its ban on holding companies, the Fair Trade Commission engaged independent scholars and launched a project to evaluate the holding company system. This report proposed that when transparency in operation management is secured, there will be a need to lift the ban on holding companies, and also suggested a few conditions for lifting the ban that could eliminate the harmful effects of holding companies.[6] Soon after, in April of 1998, the FTC organized a public-private committee to revise the Monopoly Regulation and Fair Trade Act. This committee was established following the "recommendation from the World Bank stating that an economic policy should be implemented more effectively and there is a need to improve the weaknesses that were revealed in the process of implementing the Fair Trade Law."[7] The contents in the above independent report and the recommendation from the public-private committee were used as a reference when the FTC drew up the revised Fair Trade Law. The M&A Division of the FTC drew up a restricted permission plan for holding companies in April of 1998 (Fair Trade Commission 1998a). The aim of the restricted ban lift was to "utilize the proper function of holding companies in supporting the smooth promotion of restructuring for concentrating the core competencies of companies." The proposal restrictively lifted the ban on holding companies: (1) it limited the debt ratio of holding companies to 100%, prohibiting direct cross investment between holding companies and subsidiary companies; (2) it mandated a share ratio of holding companies to subsidiary companies of over 50%; (3) it prohibited simultaneous ownership of financial subsidiary companies and non-financial subsidiary companies; and (4) it completely resolved the debt guarantees of the top 30 conglomerates (Fair Trade Commission, April 28, 1998b).

In the process of preparing the revised Fair Trade Law, bureaucratic politics within government departments were not absent. The Ministry of Finance and Economy abolished the regulation requiring holding companies to maintain a debt ratio of no greater than 100%, allowing for the free borrowing of foundation funds, and proposed to set the lower limit of the shareholding rate of holding companies to higher than 50%. This is known to have reflected the demands raised in the meeting

---

[6]The research "Evaluation and Improvement Measures for South Korea's Prohibition on Holding Companies (1998)" seems to have generally referred Japan's proposal to lift its ban on holding companies.

[7]The committee operated temporarily and its membership consisted of the following: 4 members from government departments including the Assistant Deputy Minister of the Ministry of Finance and Economy and 11 members from academia, private companies, and research institutes.

held between the CEOs of the top 5 conglomerates and economic bureaucrats on July 26, 1998 (*The Korea Economic Daily*, July 29, 1998b).[8]

In April of 1998, the Ministry of Commerce, Industry and Energy requested the FTC to permit holding companies without restrictions in the case of restructuring firms and to promote restructuring and tax incentives and President Kim Dae-jung agreed to this. The FTC's decision to hastily prepare a revised proposal to allow a restricted lift of the ban on holding companies, which was a turnaround from their previous opposing stance, can be interpreted as a response to internal concerns that if the FTC continued to stick to its opposition, the leadership over the issue of holding companies may go to the MOCIE (*Maeil Business News*, April 20, 1998b). Moreover, the MOCIE had recently advocated industry's position, emphasizing a paradigm shift of government policy from a supervisory function to an adjudicatory function, and determined that the conditions for the establishment of holding companies needed to be relaxed in order to build an efficient industrial structure (*The Korea Economic Daily*, December 18, 1998e). For the MOCIE, it was a strategy to reappear as an economic policy planning department rather than simply a regulatory organization.

MOCIE's strategy was a movement that could threaten the FTC. A competition structure among departments was formed. So, even just to cancel this out, the FTC had no choice but to take an aggressive pro-legalization stance, although the position it took maintained restrictions on holding companies. In addition to this, there were other sporadic occurrences of bureaucratic politics between bureaucrat departments surrounding economic policy. In the summer of 1997, in the midst of the dispute over lifting the ban on financial holding companies, although the MOFE did not oppose permitting financial holding companies to exist, it was, at the same time, concerned about the reduction in tax revenues that would occur in the process of introducing financial holding companies. Thus, it took a passive position towards institutional change (*Joongang Ilbo*, July 3, 1997a).

Meanwhile, there were conflicts of attribution between the FTC and the Ministry of Justice surrounding the introduction of a dual system modeled after the US, where the prosecution holds the rights to suits in civil and criminal cases, and the contesting authorities also hold the rights to suits to strengthen sanctions towards violating competition law. There was also a jurisdictional dispute between the FTC and the MOCIE surrounding the dispute over whether introducing competition-restrictive industrial policy without prior consultation with the Fair Trade Commission was in violation of the Monopoly Regulation and Fair Trade Act.

---

[8] With this proposal from the Ministry of Finance and Economy, the submission of a revised Fair Trade Act to the Cabinet council was delayed, and the executive directors of both departments renegotiated the matter.

Although there were demands from academia, civil groups, and business circles at public hearings (*The Korea Economic Daily*, September 17, 1998c),[9] the first revised bill by the FTC was accepted without changes. The president carefully watched the progress of *chaebol* reform to schedule the holding company system. At the National Congress for New Politics (NCNP) officiated party briefing in September 23rd 1998, president Kim Dae-jung instructed to "review *chaebol* restructuring" (*The Korea Economic Daily*, September 21, 1998d). As the direction of top 5 conglomerates' restructuring was determined at the meeting between political and business worlds on December 7, 1998, Kim Won-gil, the chairman of the NCNP policy committee, declared that there was no reason to delay lifting the ban on holding companies, and announced that implementation would start in 1999 (*Joongang Ilbo*, December 8, 1998b). This debate between the president and the political world was greatly influenced by the advice of the World Bank. An NCNP policy committee member confirmed that "considering resistance from civil groups, the establishment of holding companies should have been deferred. However, the Kim Dae-jung government permitted the holding companies system to reflect advice by the World Bank (*The Korea Economic Daily*, September 17, 1998c).

Labor organizations such as the Federation of Korean Trade Unions (FKTU) and the Korean Confederation of Trade Unions (KFTU) argued for *chaebol* reform but they did not express an official view on lifting the ban on holding companies. Also, because their opposing views were not elaborated, the Kim Dae-jung government did not reflect the views of the People's Solidarity for Participatory Democracy (PSPD) in the policymaking process. On the contrary, the FTC faithfully followed the president's instructions to push for a restricted lifting of the ban and strengthen its organization. The World Bank argued that instead of legalizing holding companies, the FTC's investigation right should be strengthened. The World Bank advocated that in order to strongly restrict the anti-competitive behavior of *chaebol*, the power to search and confiscate should be given to the FTC (*Chosun Ilbo*, October 4, 1998b). Despite opposition from the business world, the FTC, supported by such external pressure, secured the right to chase the financial accounts of businesses suspected of engaging in anti-competitive behavior.

The desire to stimulate the economy and strengthen political power also worked as an impetus behind the Kim Dae-jung government's decision. The Kim Dae-jung administration remained caught in the dilemma. One the one hand it demanded *chaebol* reform. On the other hand, it had to stimulate the economy by encouraging *chaebol* investment. A rapid economic revitalization was desperately needed to overcome the serious recession that followed the economic crisis and to recover social stability. The Kim Dae-jung administration had to find a middle ground in the collision between policy ideas and interests. Furthermore, the legalization of holding companies was aligned with the interests of foreign investors and international

[9] At the public hearing held by the NCNP policy committee on September 17th, 1998, the People's Solidarity for Participatory Democracy (PSPD) clearly expressed an opposing position, stating that "if pure holding companies are permitted, the ceiling on gross amount of investment needs to be revived in a limited fashion to prevent the dangers of a joint operating holding company."

financial institutions. For foreign investors, the policy idea and interests regarding the legalization of holding companies matched exactly.

Eventually, despite the large gap between the government and foreign investors in terms of the policy ideas on holding companies, the holding companies system was legalized as the interests of the Kim Dae-jung government, foreign investors and international financial institutions, and *chaebol* converged. Under the situation where South Korean society and the Kim Dae-jung government continued to hold a negative policy idea towards holding companies, implementing a restrictive lift of the ban on holding companies proved an optimal middle ground for all relevant interest groups.

2.4 Regulatory Politics on the Gross Amount of Investment: Various Matches of Policy Ideas and Interests

2.4.1 Divergent Policy Ideas Among Domestic Actors

According to Article 9 of the Fair Trade Act, any company belonging to an enterprise group shall not acquire or own stocks of an affiliated company exceeding a certain ratio of its net assets. This provision shall not apply to state-owned companies, holding companies, or foreign companies. It was one of the key regulations of Monopoly Regulation and Fair Trade Act that the South Korean government introduced in 1987 to prevent economic concentration among the top 30 large conglomerates. The investment limit within the same group was relaxed from 40% to 25% of a parent company's net assets in 1994. However, in February of 1998, right after the economic crisis, the South Korean government abolished the limit to protect the management rights of South Korean companies and to induce restructuring as a countermeasure to the M&A of foreign companies. In April of 2001, the Kim Dae-jung administration revived the investment limit following a resurgence of the harmful effects of the diversified management of *chaebol* and a deepening of economic concentration. However, in March of 2009, the limit was again discontinued due to the continued opposition of *chaebol* as they argued it was anachronistic in the age of deregulation and globalization. Until now, the limit is a distinctive regulation that uniquely exists in South Korea. With the deepening economic concentration of *chaebol* and consequently strengthened anti-*chaebol* sentiment from the people, there are voices demanding the reintroduction of the limit.

The South Korean government's policy idea regarding this regulation was in total opposition to the policy idea held by the *chaebol*. The government considered the regulation on the gross amount of investment to be essential in preventing unrelated diversification strategies and to lower economic concentration. The government and civil society shared the idea that market competition was impeded by *chaebol* monopolies. It was also thought that the increased debt of the *chaebol* may endanger the national economy. It is true that the heavy chemical industrialization strategy which started in 1972 brought about compressed growth. However, the people and the government had historical memories regarding *chaebol* of monopoly, duplicated investment, and the liquidation of repeatedly insolvent enterprises through injections of tax payer money, which were the background behind these strengthened restraints on the gross amount of investment.

On the contrary, large conglomerates had the policy idea that the investment of a company should be determined by the company, and the government should not control it. They also believed that deregulation helps strengthen the competitiveness of companies and the overall development of the national economy. In *chaebol*'s view, the regulation not only hinders efficient allocation of resources, but also causes government failure and inefficiency. *Chaebol* argued that restraints on the gross amount of investment hinders the ability of existing companies to expand investment through takeovers. The regulation also makes it difficult to enter a new market such as the high-tech industry that is relatively high risk because entry into such industries requires a large initial capital investment. They also claimed that if a foreign company that is free to invest in domestic companies attempts a hostile M&A, it is difficult to defend management rights. The government's policy idea towards this system is natural considering South Korea's experience of adhering to a state-interventionist industrialization strategy, and its institutional and cultural inertia. It was difficult to close the gap between the policy ideas of the two groups. This gap has persisted since the early 1960s, when South Korea embarked on its developmental state modeled economic growth.

Foreign investors and international financial institutions did not have a particular policy idea or interest in South Korea's peculiar restrictions on the gross amount of investment. First of all, the regulation did not apply to foreign investors operating in the South Korean market and was only enforced for domestic large conglomerates. The regulation would not influence the activities of foreign investors in the South Korean market. Foreign investors shared similar policy ideas with *chaebol* groups in that they should respect international rules on deregulation. However, foreign investors and international financial institutions thought that most harmful effects such as the opaqueness and monopoly of *chaebol* would be resolved if the corporate governance structure improved through the introduction of a consolidated accounting system and strengthened competition policy. Because the interests of foreign investors in this regulation were neither clear nor certain, they did not apply external pressure towards institutional change.

However, policy ideas do not operate in the political vacuum and are not realized into specific polices without modifications. Depending on the timing, stage of policy, and certain other issues, policy ideas can sometimes coincide or discord with the interests of actors. Policy ideas are expressed in specific policies or institutions after interacting with the various interests of actors. Foreign investors did not have any interests that would have led them to pressure the South Korean government to relax regulations regarding the changing direction and content of restrictions on the gross amount of investment. The regulation neither matched the policy ideas of foreign investors, nor disturbed their specific interests. Foreign investors did not make concrete actions the South Korean government to relax regulations, the regulation did not generate direct influence on foreign investors.

2.4.2 Changing Interest Alignments Among Domestic Actors Over Time

Before the crisis, there was a widely held presumption that the government implicitly guaranteed to eliminate risks for *chaebol* investments. In one sense, this policy had the right intention of trying to limit *chaebol* from over indulging in moral hazard, which foreign investors would certainly see as desirable. In another sense, such a discretionary restriction on investment can only be interpreted as just another heavy-handed intervention by the government to arbitrarily alter market outcomes. As the theory of policy reform tells us, policy reform measures should always try to get at the source of the problem, not just mask its symptoms. In this sense, it is not analytically apparent as to whether restrictions on the gross amount of investment actually would help contain the *chaebol* problem, or make the problem even worse. At very least, such a measure can be seen as an outright intervention that adds a regulatory burden to the economy, contradicting the principle of free and open competition. In sum, the interest and ideas of foreign investors cannot be identified with clarity regarding this institutional reform agenda.

In a structure where external pressure does not act in the specific process of institutional change, convergence or divergence of the interests between the domestic actors shapes the direction of change and width of the shift in the ceiling on the gross amount of investment. The incentive structure and interests of a particular period and the policy ideas of conflicting actors determined the method of how policy ideas are reflected in institutional change. The interests of domestic actors have been reflected more strongly than the voice and interests of foreign investors. Since the interests and voices of foreign stakeholders rarely came into view, no interest alignment and policy coalition directed by foreign investors and international financial institutions could be formed in the process of institutional change regarding this specific agenda.

After the financial crisis, the Korean government had initially eliminated the previous restrictions on gross investment. While this action could be interpreted as pro-globalization measure, a deeper reason behind it was the government's desire to provide the *chaebol* with a level playing field by giving them a way to protect themselves against hostile takeovers by international investors. In the process of the 1997 economic reform, the Kim Dae-jung administration promoted a reform strategy based on neo-liberalism. The Kim Dae-jung administration used to prefer a development strategy led by the middle class and small and medium-sized enterprises, while restraining the *chaebol* market monopoly. However, in the middle of a sovereign default, it could only accept the neo-liberal policy ideas demanded by the IMF and international capital. President Kim also abolished the restrictions on the gross amount of investment from a realistic need to stimulate the economy, and could not remain a spectator in the midst of the domino of *chaebol* bankruptcies. At the time, even the civic groups that held anti-*chaebol* sentiment did not oppose the abolishment of the regulation on the gross amount of investment under the economic nationalist policy idea of not allowing South Korean companies to be sold to foreign corporations at dirt cheap prices, and opposing the drain of national wealth.

However, after the restriction was repealed, the gross investment of *chaebol* subsidiaries continued to increase and a growing criticism emerged saying that *chaebol* reform had retreated. The ratio of investment rates in the 30 largest conglomerates increased from 29.8% in 1998 to 35.65% in 2001. Moreover, liquidity problems faced by Daewoo and Hyundai Electronics at that time placed a lot of political pressure on the Kim Dae-jung administration. At the same time, the Kim Dae-jung administration faced limited options because it would not be possible to recover from the recession and complete corporate restructuring efforts without help from the *chaebol*. The government simply could not tie the hands of the *chaebol* again. Hence, the government underwent its most drastic program of deregulation ever while at same time trying to maintain the principles of *chaebol* reform. The compromise reached then in the Fair Trade Act was to allow many exclusionary clauses in the Regulation on the Gross Amount of Investment and allow deferment for 3 years. The eventual outcome was that, although restrictions were resurrected in April 2001, they did not have a real impact on regulating *chaebol* activities (Table 2.1).

During this process, *chaebol*/the opposition party and the government/the ruling party held opposing interest alignments. *Chaebol* and opposition party in favor of deregulation aligned to repeal or incapacitate the restrictions on the gross amount of investment. The Grand National Party (GNP), the opposition party at the time, was a party that represented the interests of the *chaebol*. By contrast, the government and the ruling party, an anti-deregulation policy coalition, came together to limit the *chaebol* to break the myth of "too big to fail" by tightening the restrictions on *chaebol* investment. The ruling Millennium Democratic Party (MDP) originally had the policy idea of opposing *chaebol* monopolies. Civil society, which held strongly anti-*chaebol* sentiments, also put strong pressures on the Kim Dae-jung administration to promote *chaebol* reforms.

Why did the Kim Dae-jung administration reintroduce a regulation that contradicted *chaebol* reform in April 2001? First of all, after the economic crisis, the Kim administration was at a critical juncture where they could only accept the neo-liberal measures to relax regulations. But Kim Dae-jung's policy idea, as summarized in the so-called mass economy theory, emphasized democratic control of the economy (Rhyu 2013). As South Korea repaid all of its debt to the IMF in one and a half years, Kim Dae-jung's longstanding policy idea of regulating *chaebol* began to influence government policies. Furthermore, immediately after the financial crisis, when the IMF, which formed an axis of Kim Dae-jung's policy coalition, exited, Kim Dae-jung's political interests in reshuffling and strengthening regulations formed a policy coalition with the anti-chaebol South Korean civil society.

The Kim Dae-jung administration desperately needed a strategy to strengthen his political foundation, facing a reality where the fruits of economic reform did not directly benefit the middle class or the people despite the smooth progress of the economic reform. In his Independence Day speech in 1999, Kim Dae-jung emphasized the necessity of *chaebol* reform by saying the following: "The five principles promoted for *chaebol* reform – improvement of transparency, settlement of cross payment guarantees, specialization of industry, and strengthening of management accountability – should be completed without a failure. Moreover, the financial

Table 2.1 The political process of institutional change concerning the restriction on the gross amount of investment (1997–2003)

Time	Major Interactions and Interest Alignments Among Related Actors
September, 1997	The Federation of Korean Industries requested that the government and the ruling party (Grand National Party) remove the restriction.
February, 1998	The Kim Dae-jung government abolished the restriction just after the Asian Crisis to help with *chaebol* reform. It helped *chaebol* easily participate in corporate restructuring, encouraged competition through easy M&A, and protected management control of domestic firms from hostile takeovers by foreign investors.
August 17, 1998	The Fair Trade Commission considered the restoration of the restriction from the lessons of Daewoo bankruptcy and growing caution regarding *chaebol* expansion.
August 25, 1999	President Kim Dae-jung declared an agreement on the reintroduction of the restriction after a Blue House meeting between President and Chairmen of major *chaebol*.
August 31, 1999	The Federation of Korean Industries requested a loosening of the ceiling to 25% and a grace period of 3 years.
September 9, 1999	The ruling party (People's Council for New Politics) and the Fair Trade Commission agreed on the revision of Fair Trade Law (investment limit of up to 25%, with a grace period of dissolution of overinvested amount of 1 year). The bill tightening regulations passed the National Assembly on December 1, 1999.
February, 2000	*Chaebol* requested an exception for venture industry investment and the acquisition of newly privatized firms.
April, 2001	The Regulation on Gross Amount of Investment was finally reintroduced after the political dynamics between pro-policy coalition and anti-policy coalition.
May, 2001	Policy confrontation and interest competition between the ruling party (New Millennium Democratic Party, renamed on January 20, 2000) and the opposition party restarted. The opposition party, whose interests were strongly aligned with that of *chaebol*, requested a re-abolition of the regulation.
May 15, 2001	The Kim Dae-jung government and the ruling party proclaimed the so-called 'flexible application' of the regulation.
September 4, 2001	The ruling party demanded the government do an extensive deregulation of *chaebol* in order to overcome the economic depression, which was a political compromise to meet the growing pressure from *chaebol* and economic imperative.
November, 2001	The Kim Dae-jung government turned the policy line to deregulation and flexible enforcement. The ownership over 25% was only deprived of voting rights without selling off their ownership stake.
January, 2002	The Fair Trade Law (Monopoly Regulation and Fair Trade Act) was amended to allow 19 exception clauses and a 3-year deferment period.
April, 2004	The Fair Trade Commission amended the enforcement ordinance of the Monopoly Regulation and Fair Trade Act, which offered *chaebol* huge relief on regulations. 19 *chaebol* groups were exempted from regulations.

domination of *chaebol* through subsidiary financial companies will be prevented. *Chaebol* reform can only succeed with the prevention of the financial domination of industrial capital. Cross-share holding and unfair inside transactions will be deterred, and irregular successions will be stopped thoroughly. I will become the first president in Korean history to reform the *chaebol*, and restore the economy to center on the middle class" (Kim Dae-jung Presidential Library and Museum 2015).

The ruling MDP's defeat in the 16th general elections in April 2000 was a trigger for Kim Dae-jung to further emphasize *chaebol* reform. This election served as an interim evaluation of the economic reform and economic stimulation policies of the Kim Dae-jung administration. The Kim Dae-jung administration underwent some self-reflection and concluded that the people were not actually feeling the benefits of the Kim government's economic reforms. The administration also perceived that the electors withdrew their support because they were disappointed that the spirit and principle of *chaebol* reform was destroyed. The election results were a big loss for the Kim Dae-jung government, and it went against their crucial interests. In order to avoid a situation where their interests were threatened again, the Kim Dae-Jung government reintroduced its restrictions on the gross amount of investment in April 2001. However, the degree to which the newly introduced ceiling on the gross amount of investment was determined according to the political economic interests that the Kim Dae-jung government pursued.

The political imperative to revitalize the domestic economy was also an important factor in facilitating institutional changes toward extensive deregulation. In October of 2001, Lee Nam-gi, the Minister of the FTC, stated that the relaxation of *chaebol* reform was unavoidable due to the serious economic depression. This indicates that domestic political logic and interests strongly influenced the institutional change mechanism. Under the circumstance, *chaebol* continued to demand relief from regulations and pressured the government to make the regulations ineffective. Bureaucratic politics took place within the government. The MOFE and the Ministry of Industry and Energy (MIC) preferred that these regulations be flexibly applied, due to their concerns over the need to revitalize the economy and placate the interests of the *chaebol*. The FTC held strongly to its position due to its organizational interest as a major agency responsible for monitoring the *chaebol*. In this process, the voice of civil society was nearly absent.

The ceiling on the gross amount of investments was finally officially abolished again in March 2009 under the Lee Myung-bak administration that hailed globalization and deregulation as a new political agenda. As the political grip on *chaebol* weakened, the power of *chaebol* within the domestic political economy strengthened, consequently leading to the eventual repeal of the regulation restricting the gross amount of investment. Ultimately, regulatory changes in the gross amount of investment is another example where the pattern and direction changed according to how ideas and interests combined in concrete political processes. An examination of this case confirms that while conflicts between the two policy coalitions existed, the shifting interests over time resulted in repeated institutional change. The Kim Dae-jung administration's dilemma between siding with the people's propensity towards strong anti-*chaebol* sentiment and the need to strengthen its weakened policy coalition with civil society, and siding with the economic interests that can only borrow the power of *chaebol* to revitalize the economy created ongoing tension, and the interactions between these two sides resulted in shifts between regulation and deregulation.

2.5 Deregulation of the 4 Percent Rule: Interest Alignments Between the President and *Chaebol*

2.5.1 Traditional Policy Ideas on Competition Policy in the Financial Market

The question of whether separation of industrial capital and financial capital should be repealed has been an issue for a long time. The current regulation that separates industrial and financial capital originated in Venice banks in Medieval Europe, where regulations prohibited them directly trading in copper, tin, and iron. At the time, there were also concerns that banks would monopolize trade. The regulations on fusing financial with industrial capital vary in each country according to its perspective on the role of the finance industry and banks, power relations, and historical experiences. Germany completely permits this fusion, as it perceives the role of banks to be that of a long term investor helping to stabilize industrial capital rather than that of an institution pursuing private gains.

On the contrary, in the US, with the introduction of the 1993 Glass-Steagall Act, and the 1956 Bank Holding Company Act, strong regulations were maintained to reduce the damage from the fusion of industrial capital with financial capital. However, regulations go through cycles of tightening or relaxation depending on changes in government policy ideas or the outbreak of an economic crisis. Currently, industrial capital is limited to owning 25% of financial capital. However, in the US, it is still prohibited for banks to own non-financial industries.

In the UK, there is no direct limit of ownership regarding shares in banks, but when a non-financial company becomes a controller holding more than 10% of bank stocks, according to the Financial Services and Markets Act, it must go through an eligibility screening by the FSA. Japan also permits direct cross-shareholding between the manufacturing industry and financial industry, but the limit of ownership is regulated to not exceed 5%. In contrast to South Korea, the purpose of this policy in Japan is to prevent the traditionally larger and stronger financial conglomerates from owning industrial conglomerates. All countries in the world are commonly aware of the possible harmful effects that the monopolization of industrial capital and financial capital can bring about.

South Korea is one of the countries that is most proactive in its regulation of the fusion of financial and industrial capital. In 1995, South Korea introduced a system that strongly regulates this fusion by preventing it from occurring in advance. According to the Banking Act, "No non-financial business operator may hold more than 4/100 of the total number of outstanding voting stocks of a bank (15/100 in cases of a local bank), if a non-financial business operator obtains approval from the Financial Services Commission for stocks of a bank he/she intends to hold beyond the limit set out on the condition that he/she will not exercise his/her voting rights in the stocks... he/she may hold such stocks up to [10/100], [those of the financial or insurance company shall not exceed 15/100 of the gross number of stocks issued by the said affiliated company]." Despite many debates in the meantime, the separation rule, which was maintained under the policy idea of preventing the financial domination of *chaebol*, was changed during the Lee Myung-bak administration to raise the limit of ownership from 4% to 9%. What made such a sudden institutional change possible? In particular, why was such institutional change possible, even in a situation which, unlike the 1997 financial crisis, lacked strong external pressure to deregulate?

The core of South Korea's traditional economic model lies in government-led economic development strategies and resource allocation through government-controlled credit allocation. The South Korean developmental state can be summarized as the allocation of policy finance through banks that are controlled by the government and discretionary monetary policy by bureaucrats. For a long time before actual industrialization began, South Korea did not have a well-developed private financial ecosystem. Most financial institutions started out as public enterprises, and even after privatization, at least until the 1997 economic crisis, were continually managed by the direct intervention of the government. Traditionally, there were insufficient financial resources, so there was a clear limitation on the role of private companies supplying capital to the market. The government always had to directly provide important funding. In this way, there was strong perception of the financial industry and banks as a public good. The financial industry was perceived not as a subject of investment to make a profit, but as a public policy tool to support the national economy and economic growth.

The South Korean government nurtured the *chaebol* as an engine of economic growth. But it was intolerable for *chaebol* to dominate banks. Ownership of banks by *chaebol* would damage the public nature of the banks, and it could only be perceived as a private company interfering in the government arena. South Korea's economic growth model, and the unique relationship of government-*chaebol*-bank implied in this model, became the background of the policy idea that strictly controlled the fusion of industrial and financial capital. Major civil activist groups with strong anti-*chaebol* sentiments shared a similar policy idea with the government. The core policy idea to strengthen the separation of financial and industrial capital is that if the separation of industrial and financial capital is relaxed, *chaebol* can turn banks into their private vaults. And because *chaebol* could concentrate loans towards their loan subsidiary companies, it would lead to heightened economic concentration and hindering competition in the financial market. This would likely eventually damage the rights and interests of the national economy, financial consumers, and the people.

Foreign investors do not have a consistent policy idea regarding separation of financial capital and industrial capital. Some countries allow for the fusion of financial and industrial capital, and even if a country regulates it, there is a wide variation on the limits of ownership. There is not a particular policy idea towards South Korea's regulation policy apart from the general rule from the perspective of the rule of market economy and neo-classicalism that competition in the financial market should not be hindered, and that government-led credit allocation should not continue.

When *chaebol* power in the South Korean market strengthened from the early 1980s, *chaebol* began to have the policy idea of opposing direct intervention of the government and emphasizing market autonomy. They began to promote this specific ideology to make it the dominate policy idea in South Korean society. It is an undeniable fact that *chaebol* engaged in various political activities such as lobbying and applying political pressure in order to push for cooperation between the National Assembly and bureaucrats to make institutional changes to their advantage. There was no special reason for international capitalists to oppose *chaebol* policy ideas supporting market autonomy and the reduction of government intervention. The *chaebol* policy idea of abolishing regulations regarding the separation of financial and industrial capital is rooted in the logic that if the state does not follow global standards and step away from the market, and regulation of separation of financial and industrial capital is not repealed, South Korea's finance industry will be unable to improve its competitiveness, and eventually it will not help the national economy or the interests of the consumer. *Chaebol* and the policy coalition that supports their policy ideas argued that the matters that the government is concerned about are already monitored through other regulations, so the regulation of the separation of financial and industrial capital is redundant. They also argued that it is reverse discrimination to allow 10% for foreign capital while limiting South Korean industrial capital only to 4%. Furthermore, the deregulation policy coalition argued that the genuine intentions of the government are to maintain ongoing control over the banks and sustain the regulatory power of bureaucrats.

2.5.2 Interest Alignments Between the President and Capitalists

Why was there sudden change in deregulation under the Lee Myung-bak administration despite the government's possession of a strong policy idea regarding the separation of financial and industrial capital? The international comparison does not suggest that deregulation under the Lee Myung-bak government completely changed the traditional policy idea regarding the separation of financial and industrial capital. There was a relaxation on the ownership limit, but the rule of separation of financial and industrial capital did not fundamentally change, and the government's direct control over banks was maintained using a variety of channels. Under the Park Geun-hye administration, every time a major financial incident or *chaebol* insolvency became a social problem, strong voices were raised arguing for a retightening of the separation of financial and industrial capital in both the opposition and the ruling parties.

In addition, after the 2008 global financial crisis, 2009 was a period when almost all countries in the world, including the US, tightened financial regulations. However, South Korea underwent a sudden institutional change in the opposite direction, which is quite interesting. What made such deregulation possible? In short, this sudden institutional change was brought about by the interest alignment of President Lee Myung-bak with the *chaebol* at a particular time. The traditional policy idea of the South Korean government did not completely change, but President Lee Myung-bak's personal policy ideas and interests neutralized traditional policy ideas, resulting in institutional change along a particular pattern and path.

Disputes regarding the separation of financial and industrial capital were first formed in October of 2003 after Lone Star took over Korea Exchange Bank. The Roh Moo-hyun administration tried to adhere to the principle of separation of industrial and financial capital which seeks to prevent the ownership of banks by domestic *chaebol*. Interestingly, in November of 2005, Yoon Jeung-hyun, the Chairman of the Financial Service Commission, made an official remark that the principle of separation of industrial and financial capital should be relaxed.

On the background of these remarks, different views against the official view of the Roh Moo-hyun administration were suggested. The Chairman of the FSC criticized the separation of financial capital and industrial capital after Samsung group drafted the so-called 'The Roadmap for Samsung Bank' in May 2005 (Kim 2007). With the purpose of creating a Samsung financial holding company, Samsung attempted to change public opinion to favor deregulating the separation of industrial and financial capital, and a lobbying strategy. When the complete text was made public by the opposition party member Congresswoman Shim Sang-jung during the National Assembly's Strategy and Finance Committee, the political strategy of Samsung to deregulate the separation of industrial and financial capital became revealed (Suh 2011).

The remarks of the assistant Minister of MOFE, Kim Suk-dong, demonstrate that there were conflicting views among bureaucrats over the issue of separating financial capital and industrial capital. In 2005, there was a heated controversy over the issue due to the Samsung Card's violation of the law and the revision of the law to insert a penalty clause. The Chairman of the FSC made comments, supporting stakeholders with similar views including the director of the Bank of Korea and the presidents of domestic major banks and financial institutions, and representatives of opposition parties (e.g. the Grand National Party).

As can be seen in this case, despite having the policy idea of the separation of industrial and financial capital, the Roh Moo-hyun administration failed to control bureaucrats in the actual process of policy implementation and was not free from Samsung's lobby and political influence. Lawmaker Hong Jong-hak pointed out that because the ruling Uri Party and the Democratic Party had problems as there were few legislators interested in *chaebol* issues, president alone could not take the lead in *chaebol* policy (Table 2.2).

The Roh Moo-hyun administration's failure acted as a favorable factor in the Lee Myung-bak government's relaxation policy of the separation of industrial and financial capital. In his public speech at the National Assembly, president Lee, with his presidential election pledge to ease the separation of financial capital and industrial capital contrary to President Roh, requested cooperation in passing the bills for the revision of the 4 percent rules. It was quite an exceptional case that the president

Table 2.2 The political process of easing regulations on the separation of industrial capital and financial capital in Korea (2005–2009)

Time	Major Interactions and Interest Alignments Among Related Actors
November, 2005	Yoon Jeung-hyun, the Chairman of the Financial Service Commission (FSC), mentioned that it is necessary to consider using industry capital for the financial industry.
February, 2006	In relation to the Lone Star's KEB sale plan, Yoon Jeung-hyun, the Chairman of the FSC, during a press conference announcing FSC's operation planning, mentioned the necessity of easing the regulations on the separation of financial capital and industrial capital again with intention to publicize this issue. However, the assistant minister of MOFE, Kim Suk-dong, responded negatively.
March 16, 2006	The director of the Bank of Korea, Park Seung, made a comment that it was time to reconsider easing or abolishing this kind of principle to increase domestic investment and resolve the discrimination between domestic capital and foreign capital.
March 17, 2006	Presidents of major domestic banks and financial institutions stated that domestic companies have been reversely discriminated against due to the principle of the separation of financial capital and industrial capital when selling off public fund-injected banks.
March, 2007	An independent politician, Kim Yang-soo, proposed a bill for the revision of Clause 1 of Article 16-2, which at the time limited the ownership of non-financial business operators of financial institution to 4%, to increase the limit up to 10% or 15%.
October 30, 2007	Lee Myung-bak, then presidential candidate of opposition party, Hannaradang, stated "The Korean economy can enhance its growth rate up to 7% by easing regulations on the fusion of industrial and financial capital and lowering the corporate taxes of large conglomerates" in an interview with Bloomberg TV.
February, 2008	A president-driven path of institutional change began with Lee Myung-bak administration.
April 22, 2008	Samsung Group announced the 'Samsung Management Renovation Plan', which included Samsung's strategy focusing on non-banking financial businesses only. The plan stated they would not expand business to the banking industry.
October, 2008	The Chairman of the Financial Supervisory Commission, Chun Kwang-woo, mentioned during his interview that the FSC would announce a government bill on easing the separation of financial and industrial capital to be submitted to National Assembly. The bill suggested increasing the bank ownership limit for industrial capital from 4% either to 8% or to 10%. The Federation of Korean Industries (FKI) mentioned that the government bills would drive domestic financial regulations to meet the global standard and would contribute to the development of financial system and industry. The Korea Chamber of Commerce (KCCC) made a comment that the government bill would contribute to the enhanced competitiveness of domestic companies by eliminating the wall between the financial world and the industrial world for a synergy effect and urged for passage of the government bill as soon as possible. The Korea Federation of Small and Medium-sized Businesses also showed a positive reaction to the government bill, saying that it was not necessary to put restrictions on domestic industrial capital only when the market is open to foreign capital.

(continued)

Table 2.2 (continued)

Time	Major Interactions and Interest Alignments Among Related Actors
November, 2008	President Lee called, through his speech on administrative policy at the National Assembly, for non-partisan cooperation and reconfirmed with the leading members of the government and the ruling party that they would pass the so-called 'MB bills' in the upcoming regular National Assembly session, which included the revision of the Banking Act easing the separation of financial and industrial capital in a special consultative meeting.
January 6, 2009	While the UNDP agreed to make concessions to cooperate in passing the bill revising the Banking Act and the Financial Holding Company Act, the GNP agreed to accept the bill for the revision of the MRFTA, proposed by representative Hong Jae-hyung of the UNDP.
April 14, 2009	The chairmen of the Korea Federation of Banks, the Korea Life Insurance Association, and the General Insurance Association visited the National Assembly and requested passage of the bills easing the separation of financial and industrial capital.
May, 2009	The FSC proposed a revised bill for the revision of the Financial Holding Company Act to ease the ownership limit of non-financial business operator of financial institutions from 4% to 9%, in line with the revision of the Banking Act.
June, 2009	People's Solidarity for Participatory Democracy announced and criticized that the FSC brought the bill for the Financial Holding Company Act, which was rejected during the provisional session of the National Assembly in April, to the Cabinet meeting without making an 'Advance Legislation Notice'
July, 2009	The bill to revise the Financial Holding Company Act was passed in the National Assembly.

gave pressure to pass specific bills in the National Assembly (Suh 2011, 51). President Lee Myung-bak mentioned during his presidential campaign that it was necessary to ease principle of separation of financial capital and industrial capital as foreign investors have primary control over domestic banks and the policy acted as counter-discrimination against domestic capital, as observed in Lone Star's sell off of its controlling stake in Korea Exchange Bank (KEB), which it bought from majority shareholders at a fire-sale price in 2003. So relaxing the separation of financial capital and industrial capital was his major presidential election pledge. President Lee's policy idea was based on the idea of enhancing the global competitiveness of the domestic financial industry through business-friendly policies and increasing the rate of economic growth.

The Northeast Asian financial hub strategy begun with the Roh Moo-hyun government provided a positive justification for Lee Myung-bak's administration to promote deregulation in the financial industry. It worked as a justification and discourse strengthening the logic behind the Lee Myung-bak government's pledge to increase the international competitiveness of the banking industry. Although on April 22, 2008, Lee Kun-hee, the chairman of Samsung, officially announced that Samsung group would not enter into the financial industry due to growing criticism over the Samsung group's lobbying, it can only be seen as a temporary deferral strategy employed due to concerns about the large amount of capital necessary to transform into a financial holding company, and the shock of reshuffling the ownership structure. Working in close cooperation with the Samsung group since the presidential elections, president Lee Myung-bak was active in *chaebol* reform to help Samsung's entrance into the financial industry. Regardless of Samsung's declaration of renunciation, president Lee strongly pushed to ease regulations on the separation of industrial capital and financial capital based on his business friendly strategy. President Lee Myung-bak understood that the participation of *chaebol* was essential to develop South Korea's commercial banks into international investment banks and to privatize the Korea Development Bank. This, in combination with the reality that South Korea's major banks were already owned and dominated by foreign capital and after the 1997 economic crisis, resulted in the nationalistic sentiment that South Korea could not give the Korea Development Bank, which is the symbol of South Korea's financial industry, to foreign capital, also playing a role.

Policy debates surrounding the policy of separation of industrial and financial capital took the form of an interest confrontation between the regulation coalition and the deregulation coalition. The regulation policy coalition consisted of the opposition party, NGOs including PSPD and Citizens' Coalition for Economic Justice (CCEJ), labor unions, and trade unions such as KCTU and FKTU. They claimed that easing the 4 percent rules would give more economic power to *chaebol* and that banks under *chaebol* subsidiaries were likely to become private coffers, which would be contrary to the interests of the shareholders. The regulation policy coalition pursued the political interests of reclaiming political power through reducing consumer damage resulting from *chaebol* market monopolies and building up anti-*chaebol* sentiment by maintaining regulations.

The deregulation policy coalition was made up of bureaucrats (including MOFE, Financial Supervisory Authorities and the FTC), the ruling party, and domestic interest groups (including FKI, bank associations, etc.). They argued that easing the 4 percent rules would not lead to domestic banks becoming the private coffers of *chaebol* through the strict application and reviews from the institutional setting, such as reviews of the eligibility of majority shareholders (Suh 2011, 56–64). In addition, to enhance the global competitiveness of domestic banks, size matters, and combining financial and industrial capital could bring a greater synergy effect to the domestic economy. The Lee Myung-bak government had a specific interest in restructuring the government by strengthening financial competitiveness and stimulate the economy.

Given the Lee Myung-bak government's interest alignment with *chaebol* and the support from bureaucrats, the deregulation coalition had a greater number of supporting stakeholders. Bureaucratic support was largely the result of the appointment of senior economic bureaucrats who shared the same policy ideas or market views with the president himself. While the regulation coalition was scattered, the promoters and supporters of easing the separation of financial and industrial capital built a more intense interest coalition, which created a good environment for President Lee to drive his policy interests. Institutional change to ease the separation of banking and commerce was driven by this mechanism, in an abrupt and drastic pattern and path, by President Lee Myung-bak, empowered by his interest alignment with the *chaebol*.

Foreign investors did not apply any specific external pressure regarding institutional change of South Korea's separation of financial and industrial capital. After the 1997 economic crisis, the Kim Dae-jung administration strictly maintained the 4 percent ceiling, but permitted the ownership of foreign capital in South Korea's financial industry to reach 10%. However, in reality, this rule was not applied, so foreign capital in Standard Chartered Korea Limited, Citigroup Korea, KB Financial Group, Shinhan Financial Group, Hana Financial Group exceeded 50%, and in three of these banks, a non-Korean is still the majority shareholder. For the South Korean government, which was desperate for an inflow of foreign direct investment after the economic crisis, it indefinitely permitted foreign financial capital to own domestic banks because it could not apply strong regulations to foreign capital entering South Korea's financial industry.

At the time, the urgent need for inflows of foreign capital itself worked as the origin of external pressure. Because financial capital from major countries sufficiently entered South Korea's financial industry immediately following the economic crisis, there was no need to pressure for deregulation for additional entry in the process of institutional change after 2005. Furthermore, because in the US, according to their own Banking Act, banks could not possess industrial capital, US capital did not have much interest in applying additional pressure for institutional change to own South Korea's banks. Foreign capital had no interest in pressuring the South Korean government to permit the fusion of financial and industrial capital, but it had an ongoing interest in maintaining pressure on the South Korean government regarding government privileges granted to *chaebol* as an extension of government-controlled credit allocation in order to prevent *chaebol* from having an unfair competitive advantage.

In addition, traditionally, South Korea's financial industry was underdeveloped, and could not compete with international financial capital. So, even if the Lee Myung-bak administration eased the separation of financial and industrial capital and created conditions advantageous to South Korean *chaebol*, international investors were not that interested in the issue. In the same vein, President Lee Myung-bak formalized a strategy to permit *chaebol* participation in the privatization of major banks, and contain the participation of foreign capital, but it seems as though international investors did not think that the South Korean government's easing of regulations on the separation of financial and industrial capital greatly harmed their interests. In addition, in contrast to the policy ideas of Kim Dae-jung or Roh Moo-hyun, the policy idea pursued by Lee Myung-bak's administration were of creating a business friendly environment and deregulation, which was in line with the policy ideas of international capitalists emphasizing globalization and the principle of the market. Thus, international capitalists did not oppose the Lee Myung-bak government's easing of the separation of financial and industrial capital, and remained a passive actor in the policy coalition for easing regulations on the separation of financial and industrial capital.

Although South Korea's policy ideas regarding *chaebol* reform and regulations did not completely change at least under the Lee Myung-bak administration, the policy ideas regarding the separation of financial and industrial capital underwent considerable changes. Under the structure where the Lee Myung-bak government's strategy of institutional change did not seriously hinder the interests of international capital, the Lee government could achieve rapid institutional change by exploiting his interest coalition with the domestic *chaebol*. Under the situation where the interests of the president and *chaebol* coincide and foreign investors do not voice opposition, the political balance of power between the regulation policy coalition and the deregulation policy coalition collapsed, showing a drastic and abrupt pattern of institutional change.

2.6 Conclusion

This chapter shows the political process of the way in which institutional change occurred in *chaebol* reform. The legalization of holding companies was achieved through strong pressure from foreign investors and international financial institutions on the Kim Dae-jung government. Under strong external pressure, the Kim Dae-jung government could only postpone its policy ideas and follow realistic interests. This shows that the nation-state and international capital can have completely different policy ideas regarding the same institutional change issue. Policy ideas and interest relations vary within the political process of institutional change. Since foreign investors did not have a particular policy idea or interests regarding restrictions on the gross amount of investment, the policy process went through abolishment, reintroduction, neutralization, and re-abolishment.

South Korean *chaebol* reform showed a great deal of adaptive capacity in the process of institutional change. Factors such as interest alignment and convergence of policy ideas determined these various paths. When policy ideas and interests collide, it is interests rather than policy ideas that can more strongly influence institutional change. Major actors, both domestic and international, shared the same interests even if they had different policy ideas regarding a particular institutional change.

References

Acharya, Amitav. 2009. *Whose Ideas Matter? Agency and Power in Asian Regionalism*. Ithaca/London: Cornell University Press.

Ahmadjian, Christina L., and Gregory E. Robbins. 2005. A Clash of Capitalism: Foreign Shareholders and Corporate Restructuring in 1990s Japan. *American Sociological Review* 70: 451–471.

Asia Today. October 13, 2008.

Campbell, John L. 2004. *Institutional Change and Globalization*. Princeton/Oxford: Princeton University Press.

Chosun Ilbo. February 5, 1998a.

———. October 4, 1998b.

Chun, Yoon-chul. 1997. Economic Policy Direction in the Globalization Period. *Monthly Fair Competition: Fair Competition Association Magazine* 26: 2–7.
Cortell, Andrew P., and Susan Peterson. 2002. *Altered States: International Relations, Domestic Politics, and Institutional Change*. Lanham/Boulder/New York/Oxford: Lexington Books.
Dong-A Ilbo. December 16, 1998.
Fair Trade Commission. April 11, 1998a. "Press Release: Establish a Public-Private Committee to Revise of the Fair Trade Act".
———. April 28, 1998b. "Press Release: Restrictive Permission Plan of Holding Companies.".
Gourevitch, Peter A., and James J. Shinn. 2005. *Political Power and Corporate Control: The new Global Politics of Corporate Governance*. Princeton/Oxford: Princeton University Press.
Guillén, Mauro F. 2003. *The Limits of Convergence: Globalization and Organizational Change in Argentina, South Korea, and Spain*. Princeton/Oxford: Princeton University Press.
Hall, Peter A. 1989. *The Political Power of Economic Ideas: Keynesianism across Nations*. New York: Princeton University Press.
Joongang Ilbo. July 3, 1997a.
———. November 18, 1997b.
———. September 25, 1998a.
———. December 8, 1998b.
Kim Dae-jung Presidential Library and Museum. 2015. *The Complete Works of Kim Dae-jung*. Seoul: Yonsei University Press. (Korean).
Kim, Joo-yeon. October 2007. "Does the Samsung Bank Roadmap Exist?" *Monthly magazine 'Word' (Wolgan Mal)*.
Kingdon, J. 1984. *Agendas, Alternatives and Public Policies*. New York: Longman.
Kyunghyang Newspaper. September 26, 2008.
Lee, Chung H. 2005. The Political Economy of Institutional Reform in Korea. *The Journal of the Asia pacific Economy* 10 (3): 257–277.
Lee, Seungjoo, and Sang-young Rhyu. 2008. The Political Dynamics of Informal Networks in South Korea: The Case of Parachute Appointment. *The Pacific Review* 21 (1): 45–66.
Lee, Sook Jong. 2008. The Politics of Chaebol Reform in Korea: Social Cleavage and New Financial Rules. *Journal of Contemporary Asia* 38 (3): 439–452.
Leković, Vlastimir. 2011. Interaction of formal and informal institutions: impact on economic success. *Economics and Organization* 8 (4): 357–370.
Lim, Haeran. 2010. The Transformation of Developmental State and Economic Reform in Korea. *Journal of Contemporary Asia* 40 (2): 188–210.
Maeil Business News. January 20, 1998a.
———. April 20, 1998b.
Ministry of Finance and Economy, IMF Measures Task Force. February 1998. "Contents of Approval of IMF Funds Withdrawal and Declaration of Intent".
Ministry of Finance and Economy, Public Loans Task Force. September 1998. "IBRD Second Agreement on the Introduction of Structural Adjustment Loans".
Moon, Chung-in, and Sang-young Rhyu. 2010. Rethinking Alliance and the Economy: American Hegemony, Path Dependence, and the South Korean Political Economy. *International Relations of the Asia-Pacific* 10 (3): 441–464.
Nee, Victor, and Sonja Opper. 2012. *Capitalism from Below: Markets and Institutional Change in China*. Cambridge: Harvard University Press.
North, Douglass C. 1990. *Institutions, Institutional Change and Economic Performance*. New York: Cambridge University Press.
Rhyu, Sang-young. 2013. *Kim Dae-jung and Mass Economy Theory*. Seoul: Yonsei University Press.
Samsung Office of the Secretary. January 1998. "Samsung's Management Renovation Plan".
Schmidt, Vivien A. 2008. Discursive Institutionalism: The Explanatory Power of Ideas and Discourse. *The Annual Review of Political Science* 11: 303–326.

———. 2010. Taking Ideas and Discourse Seriously: Explaining Change through Discursive Institutionalism as the Fourth New Institutionalism. *European Political Science Review* 2 (1): 1–25.

———. 2012. Discursive Institutionalism: Scope, Dynamics, and Philosophical Underpinnings. In *The Argumentative Turn Revisited: Public Policy as Communicative Practice*, ed. Frank Fisher and Herbert Gottweis, 85–113. Durham/London: Duke University Press.

Seabrooke, Leonard. 2006. *The Social Sources of Financial Power: Domestic Legitimacy and International Financial Orders*. Ithaca: Cornell University Press.

Seoul Newspaper. June 25, 2007.

Steinmo, Sven, Kathleen Thelen, and Frank Longstretch, eds. 1992. *Structuring Politics: Historical Institutionalism in Comparative Perspective*. New York: Cambridge University Press.

Suh, Diane Yeonjoo. 2011. "President, Domestic Politics and Institutional Change: Deregulation of "the 4% Rule" in the Korean Financial Industry." Unpublished master thesis. Graduate School of International Studies, Yonsei University.

ten Brink, Tobias. 2011. "Institutional Change in Market-Liberal State Capitalism: An Integrative Perspective on the Development of the Private Business Sector in China." MPIfG Discussion Paper 11/ 2.

The Federation of Korean Industries. November 1998. "Corporate Governance Structure of the OECD: Position on Establishing Guidelines.". p.2.

The Korea Economic Daily. April 9, 1998a.

———. July 29, 1998b.

———. September 17, 1998c.

———. September 21, 1998d.

———. December 18, 1998e.

The United States Senate. October 2, 1998. "An Act: Making Appropriations for Foreign Operations, Export Financing, and Related Programs for the Fiscal Year Ending September 30, 1999, and for Other Purposes." Title 6 Sec. 602. http://frwebgate.access.gpo.gov.

Chapter 3
Privatization and a Lingering Developmental State: Case Studies of POSCO, KT, and Korea Development Bank

3.1 Introduction: What Shapes the Politics of Privatization?

South Korea has been classified as a typical developmental state. Centralized policymaking, vertical government-business relations, bureaucratic intervention and various industrial policies were the core of the South Korean economic development model at least until the 1997 Asian financial crisis. After the crisis, South Korea carried out a broad-scale economic reform following pressure from both inside and outside. South Korea carried out full-scale institutional reform in major areas including *chaebols*, public sector, labor, and finance. Such a series of thorough institutional reform played a positive role in helping South Korea overcome an economic crisis in a short period. It has also brought about massive change in the South Korean-type developmental state model which continued on from the 1960s. The developmental state was brought to an end in South Korea. In addition, there are views that a new post-developmental state, which moves following market principles, international standards, and transparent economic institutions, is emerging.

In the period of democratization and globalization, in South Korea, privatization was considered to be an important driving force in dismantling South Korea's developmental state, and in creating a new developmental model. It was also accepted as a core means and purpose of economic reform. Public enterprises, managed inefficiently under government protection and a monopolized market structure, were criticized as one of the causes of the 1997 economic crisis. For domestic consumers and taxpayers, public enterprises were an institution that impedes consumer benefits with low quality service and products, produce inefficiencies, and cause budget waste. For foreign investors and international financial organizations such as the IMF, South Korean public enterprises are a source of opacity, hindrance to competition, and entry barriers which discriminate against foreign enterprises.

The process and outcome of privatization could be an important barometer to transform South Korea's developmental state into a new model. However,

S. Lee and S. Rhyu, *The Political Economy of Change and Continuity in Korea*,
The Political Economy of the Asia Pacific, https://doi.org/10.1007/978-3-319-71453-0_3

privatization is not comprised of the single logic of economic calculation. Privatization goes through numerous dynamic interactions among stakeholders, constantly changing incentive structures, and real politics surrounding the allocation of power and resources. The reason why various concepts, paths, processes, and results of privatization are examined results from such political economic characteristics of privatization. What then rules the politics of privatization and the institutional change process for privatization in South Korea? Furthermore, what is the reason for the phenomenon of the developmental state being reenacted in privatized companies? This chapter attempts to provide the answer to these questions by looking at three cases of privatization: POSCO, KT, and Korea Development Bank (KDB).

The privatization of POSCO began in 1988, and was completed in 2000. A privatized POSCO showed a performance that was globally accepted during the developmental state period when the pressures of democratization and globalization were not that strong. Paradoxically, shortly following democratic consolidation and during the period when the pressure of globalization was at its peak, POSCO has faced a huge corruption scandal, inefficiency, and a decrease in competitiveness. Even further, at the beginning of 2016, POSCO recorded its first current account deficit since its establishment. It is also fully paradoxical in theory that the case of POSCO, which was regarded as an old example of completely successful privatization, fell to the property of predatory rent-seeking and increased government intervention at a time where the developmental state was weakening.

The privatization of KT began in 1998, and was concluded in 2002. KT's privatization was promoted under external pressure from foreign communication capital, and considered a measure to overcome the economic crisis immediately following 1997. However, even after KT's privatization, each new political regime has directly intervened and been involved in rent-seeking with the company. This has made KT a company with continuous large scale corruption scandals. Foreign investors' shares comprise 49% of total ownership, and the government is no longer the largest shareholder. Although KT is part of the IT industry, which endures the most pressure from technological innovation and globalization, the reality is that repeat government intervention and corruption scandals are enough evidence to question the meaning of privatization.

In the case of KDB, privatization proceeded in 2009 under the Lee Myung-bak administration, yet in 2013, the Park Geun-hye administration entirely discontinued the process as it returned to a government organization. Right after the 2008 Global financial crisis, the Lee Myung-bak administration initiated a specific privatization schedule to increase South Korea's competitiveness in the finance industry, and to strengthen investment banking. As the first step of privatization, a specific schedule to redesign related institutions by transforming KDB into a financial holding company was implemented. However, when the new administration took office, KDB reverted to its original state as a public enterprise. The political economic background and meaning of the halt of privatization of KDB, a symbol of South Korean policy finance in the developmental state period, despite criticisms from foreign investors, and pressure from globalization, is interesting.

The three cases above all differ in their periods of privatization, backgrounds, purpose, process, industry, degree of external pressure, and current management performance. However, each case shows various patterns and characteristics of privatization, especially in corporate governance structure and the influence of the state over informal institutions in South Korea. In addition, the three cases of privatization are interesting topics that show the mechanism of why the developmental state in South Korea is not disappearing, but reappearing. In this chapter, we point out the limitations of corporate governance structure and formal institutions in South Korea's process of privatization. Furthermore, the chapter investigates how the influence of domestic politics, such as the President's policy preferences, and the role played by the informal policy network rather than external pressures or economic interests, determine the process and outcome of privatization.

This chapter is organized in the following order. Part two introduces various theoretical debates on privatization and the developmental state, and proposes the research framework for this chapter. Here, to examine why privatization was not completed and failed to promote the dismantlement of development state, the research emphasizes the role of the corporate governance structure of privatized companies together with informal networks. Part three analyzes POSCO's privatization. The paradoxical phenomenon where government rent-seeking towards POSCO increased after democratization was consolidated compared to the authoritarian period will be analyzed. Part four is an examination of KT's privatization. The reason why KT has continuously encountered government intervention and been a target of corruption despite increased competition in technological innovation and external pressure towards liberalization of the communications market will be examined. Part five analyzes the plan to privatize KDB and what happened as the process foundered. It shows what caused such a phenomenon, and discusses the influence and meaning of the restoration phenomenon of South Korea's developmental state.

3.2 Contending Perspectives on Privatization and Institutional Reform

Governments usually pursue privatization in pursuit of several policy objectives. This simultaneously includes sales revenue maximization, corporate value maximization, long-term competitiveness, and other possible positive spillover effects for the rest of the economy. These political and economic objectives affect the major factors surrounding privatization decisions, such as the sales price, share allocation, control restrictions, and the design of ownership and corporate governance structure of the privatized SOE. To achieve these policy objectives, privatization must go beyond *de jure* change of ownership. Privatization cannot achieve the desired policy outcomes without *de facto* transfer of control and power from the SOE to the private sector. That is, *de facto* reduction of the discretionary power of bureaucrats and politicians must take place, in particular over privatized enterprises and over the economy. Given the institutional inertia and vested interests of related parties, however, successful transformation of SOEs into competitive privatized enterprises inevitably faces resistance. Successful privatization must often be accompanied by successful market-oriented economic reform.

Privatization means more than a change of ownership from the government or state to non-governmental entities such as individuals or commercial institutions. Boycko et al. (1996) defines privatization as a combination of two changes accompanying the change of ownership. The first involves incorporating state-owned enterprises through a turnover of control from the government to the managers of state-owned enterprises. This incorporation aims at making managers of SOEs accountable for their performance. The second change considers the transfer of cash flow ownership from the government to managers and shareholders of the enterprises. Cash flow ownership transfer intends to provide the proper incentives for managers and shareholders to act in their own interests, leading to better performance of the enterprise.

Privatization has been pursued as a cure for "government failure." Overemphasis on public interests sometimes leads SOEs or public enterprises to perform inefficiently, causing the misuse of public funds and the misallocation of scarce resources, which results in increasing tax burdens and deteriorating economic conditions. The inefficiency of public firms arises out of the agency problem associated with politicians, namely, their political discretion over public firms (Boycko et al. 1996). Political discretion can compel executives of public firms to engage in economically inefficient activities for other political objectives, such as higher levels of employment or the funneling of resources from public firms for their own private enrichment.

Does privatization work as effectively as theories predict? Mounting evidence tries to explain the effect of privatization at the micro and macroeconomic levels. As for its impact on the overall economy, empirical findings suggest that privatization itself brings mixed results. Barnett (2000) documented the relationship between privatization and fiscal and macroeconomic performance: the privatization process strongly correlates with an improvement in macroeconomic performance in the form of higher real Gross Domestic Product (GDP) growth and lower unemployment rates. On the other hand, Cook and Uchida (2001) found that privatization contributed negatively to economic growth, based on data from 63 developing countries between 1988 and 1997. Considering that (1) they analyzed only developing countries and (2) developing countries usually operate under weak regulatory regimes and within less competitive market environments, one possible explanation for their results may be that the weaknesses in implementing effective regulations and less competitive environments in developing countries may have prevented privatization from contributing to economic growth.

Nevertheless, Cook and Uchida (2001) stress that institutions really matter for the success of privatization.[1] Sachs et al. (2000) confirm the same implications concerning the importance of institutions. Based on data from 24 countries, they examined whether or not a change in ownership alone could achieve economic performance gains. They found that additional factors, such as an institution's ability to address agency issues, market competitiveness, and a regulatory framework are essential for privatization to produce positive results in economic performance. Regarding the economic impact of privatization on corporations, Megginson and Netter (2001) provided an extensive review based on 61 empirical studies assessing post-privatization performance. The findings from the review conclude that (1) privately-owned firms outperform state-owned enterprises; (2) privatization improved firm performance, regardless of the geographical setting; (3) governments generate significant resources from privatization; (4) privatization generally contributes to the development of local stock exchanges and capital markets; and (5) privatization also benefits investors who purchase shares in privatized firms.

Among empirical studies at the enterprise level, Frydman et al. (1999) and D' Souza et al. (2001) demonstrate how privatization affects performance improvement, which in turn depends upon the types of owners in the post-privatization stage. Frydman et al. (1999) found that privatization under outsider ownership resulted in performance enhancement through revenue and productivity improvement but had no significant improvement in cost efficiency. Privatization, however, had no significant impact on firms controlled by insiders (managers or employees). D' Souza et al. (2001) also found that low levels of employee ownership and high levels of foreign ownership positively correlated with stronger performance improvement. Their findings suggest that the type of ownership matters for the success of privatization. Ownership is important because different ownerships are associated with varying types of control over the corporation and different sets of incentives for managers and employees. As the above review suggests, an extensive body of theoretical and empirical research on privatization underscores the importance of institutions. Overall, the success of privatization appears to depend upon competitive market environments with a proper regulatory regime at the macroeconomic level, and good corporate governance systems and practices at the microeconomic level (Rhyu and Kim 2009, 147–150).

However, privatization cannot simply be reduced to the change of economic institutions to improve market efficiency. Bureaucratic politics and the differing policy preferences of various stakeholders complicate the process. Debates and confrontations between pro- and anti- privatization coalitions always surround the process. The corporate governance system that emerges after privatization largely depends upon the political and economic influence and dynamics of these coalitions.

[1] The critical relationship between institutions and economic reform in specific or economic performance in general has been well addressed by economists such as Douglass North and Oliver Williamson. For example, see North (1990) and Williamson (1994).

Traditionally, Korean public enterprises have played a central role in the growth of the economy under the developmental model. The influence they command has remained relatively large. Each of the controlling government ministries in turn exerted sway and control over the different public enterprises they oversaw, and bureaucrats had extensive vested rights. Bureaucrats and politicians thus tended not to support privatization measures. However, the financial crisis weakened the anti-privatization coalition and reduced its ability to resist changes. The neo-liberalism ideology to reduce the public sector in particular left the Korean government little choice but to proceed with privatization. Neo-liberalism, as symbolized by the position of the IMF as well as the aggressive efforts of Kim Dae-jung, ultimately made immediate moves towards privatization possible. When the financial crisis hit in late 1997, president-elect Kim Dae-jung had no option but to pursue serious market-oriented economic reforms of liberalization, deregulation, and privatization to achieve a fast and effective recovery from the serious economic situation. In particular, the privatization program under the Kim Dae-jung government occurred as part of the public sector reform for a "smaller and more efficient government," which privatized eleven SOEs beginning in July 1998. The objectives of the privatization program were (1) to enhance economic efficiency and improve the quality of services; (2) to reduce the extent and level of the government's direct involvement in economic activities; and (3) to direct available resources to facilitate structural adjustment programs. To this end, the government planned to transfer ownership and control of the eleven SOEs to the private sector by selling either the government's equity interests or the assets in SOEs and their subsidiaries.

The privatization program under the Kim Dae-jung government proceeded under three guiding principles: (1) early and full privatization with restructuring, if necessary; (2) fiscal revenue maximization through the best selection of sales channels and timing, and (3) priority of sales channels given to the public offering and Employee Stock Ownership Program (ESOP). The Korean government of course recognized the critical role of proper corporate governance as a prerequisite for successful and effective privatization. Therefore, they focused on providing a competitive market and regulatory environments as an external governance mechanism for the SOEs together with a proper corporate governance structure as an internal governance mechanism. As of December 2002, Korea had completely privatized eight out of eleven SOEs. To effectively expedite the privatization processes, the government revised the laws related to SOEs to make the market and regulatory environments more competitive. The Korean government also mandated that SOEs establish a corporate governance structure that held professional managers or the controlling shareholder accountable for their actions with a special emphasis on management transparency. In particular, as in the case of POSCO and KT, the privatized SOEs had to adopt professional management, with a strong board of directors, so that no single shareholder could assume control. According to one study, the overall privatization program succeeded in improving profitability, reducing costs, and improving the quality of service, yielding approximately $2 billion of fiscal revenues for the government (MPB 2002; Rhyu and Kim 2009, 15–23).

As mentioned above, South Korea's privatization, which progressed after the 1997 economic crisis, was successful according to at least a few criteria. There are several points to consider that would argue that the privatization of POSCO and KT could be analyzed as successful. First, the government sold its share to the private sector and, as a result, it is no longer the major shareholder. In addition, competition law was strengthened to promote market competition and to monitor the economic activities and products of the privatized company, and the reform of diverse formal institutions was simultaneously implemented to improve the governance structure of the newly privatized companies, with such steps as the introduction of outside directors and an auditing committee.

Another point is that the shareholder composition of foreign capital increased to approximately 50%. As of March 2016, POSCO's composition of foreign capital was approximately 53% and KT's was approximately 49%. Furthermore, through the series of economic reforms that were implemented after the 1997 Asian financial crisis, South Korea's traditional developmental state weakened. The cases of privatization are assessed as evidence leading to the dismantlement or weakening of the developmental state. South Korean domestic pressure for democratization in the economy and the market, monitoring, and pressure for transparency and accountability, and the external pressure of globalization increased. As a result, the interpretation that South Korean democracy positively influenced the management performance of privatized companies has become more persuasive.

However, the recent reality of newly privatized companies in South Korea poses fundamental questions to the conventional wisdoms listed above. First of all, during and after the process of privatization, how much of a decisive factor can formal institutions be in regulating the characteristics of a company? In the case of South Korea's privatization, the corporate governance structure was well established in terms of formal institutions. Formal institutions were introduced to increase transparency and accountability, such as outside directorship and the strengthening of protection for minority shareholders. At least at the level of a formal institution, it could be said to have complied with the so-called global standard. POSCO and KT's corporate governance structures were assessed as high by many international credit evaluation agencies and financial institutions.

Despite formal institutional changes, in South Korea's privatized companies, informal institutions have a greater influence than formal institutions. There are many cases where informal institutions, such as informal networks and political pressure, have incapacitated formal institutions. As in the cases of Enron and Lehman Brothers, in any country in the world, there are many cases where well organized corporate governance structure cannot play its role and limitations of formal institutions are revealed regardless as to whether the company is a private one or a public enterprise. In this sense, South Korea is not an exception. But in South Korea, it is unique that informal institutions determine the path and outcome of privatization and economic reform (Rhyu and Lee 2006). With informal institutions not entirely dissolving, not the substance but the form of South Korea's privatization and economic reform converge to meet global standards, bringing about a problem of mock-compliance. Informal networks acted as the biggest element that made the privatized POSCO and KT degenerate back into a target of political pressure and government intervention.

Secondly, privatization is simultaneously a key policy achievement created by the pressure of globalization and a core policy of the Washington Consensus. So, it is a policy example that is most sensitive to globalization and democratization. Nevertheless, in a period where globalization and democratization are heightening, why and how are domestic politics and the political choices of the president having a bigger influence than either of these factors in South Korea's privatization? All political economic debates surrounding the institutional change process can be summed up as the controversy between globalization versus nation state, and there have been numerous disputes and research regarding this subject. Recent theoretical arguments are mainly focused on identifying the various interactions and paths of how globalization in different countries and cases passes through the process of state mediation and shows up as the outcome of institutional change in a host country, and how the nation-state adopts to the pressure of globalization (Keohane and Milner 1996; Walter 2008). Debates on developmental state and post-developmental state occur in the same context. After the Asian Financial Crisis, there has been active discussion about the ending of South Korea's developmental state. However, it has been seen that the developmental state is being revived in privatized companies. The path of privatization was determined by domestic politics, particularly by the policy preferences of the president and political interests or demands, rather than by the external pressures of globalization or market power. Repeated predatory rent-seeking in POSCO and KT occurs to serve the political interests of the ruling coalition centered on the President. The sudden cancelation of KDB's privatization plan and its return to a public enterprise was done according to the policy choice of the president in consideration of domestic politics. The lack of a role available to foreign owners, regardless of the high proportion of foreign ownership in these companies, was also a clear limitation in protecting privatized companies from political rent-seeking. This is an example that demonstrates that the path of institutional change in South Korea can be determined by domestic politics and the policy choices of the president, rather than by economic elements such as globalization and market pressure.

3.3 POSCO: A Paradoxical Success of Privatization

Founded in 1968, POSCO has been one of the favored candidates for privatization since its early days, beginning in the 1970s. The Ministry of Finance (MOF) first planned to privatize the company in 1976 as part of a policy initiative to increase Korea's fiscal revenues and develop its financial markets. However, conflicts between various ministries delayed the actual implementation of this plan for over 12 years. The Ministry of Commerce and Industry (MCI), in particular, preferred to delay and adopt a gradual privatization through which the government would remain the controlling majority shareholder, while the Ministry of Finance pushed to expedite the POSCO privatization process (Rhyu 1996). After an extended delay arising from these conflicts between holders of different policy objectives, the MOF of Korea again proposed privatizing POSCO and selling off the shares owned by the government and commercial banks to buyers off the stock market in 1987. The MOF argued that off-the-market privatization would effectively maximize the revenue from the privatization and restore calm to the local stock market. POSCO's management team and the MCI, however, opposed MOF's proposal. After a year-long delay arising from this conflict, a privatization plan was created that left 35% of the shares held by the government and Korea Development Bank, selling 27% of the shares through a public offering, and allocating 10% of the shares to the ESOP. Before the partial sell-off through a public offering and ESOP, the Korean government also passed laws that effectively blocked the emergence of a controlling shareholder. The Korean government remained *de jure* controlling shareholder of POSCO before the complete turnover of the ownership to the private sector. This controlling position notwithstanding, POSCO began to gradually enjoy more autonomy. Nevertheless, POSCO management continued to fear not only government interference into management but also a takeover by a *chaebol*. They believed this would destabilize its world class management.[2] Chairman Park Tae-joon and his management team always argued that POSCO's management possessed expertise and integrity and would perform best without outside interference. In fact, even while it technically remained an SOE, the management team achieved impressive performances in making POSCO globally competitive.

The second round of POSCO's privatization began under the Kim Young Sam government in 1994. This privatization sought to establish an autonomous professional management group monitored and supervised by a strong board of directors and shareholders associations with a dispersed ownership structure. MOF wanted an expedited sale of as many government shares as possible to the private sector. POSCO's management team also favored this type of privatization policy, chiefly with the remaining shares to be sold to POSTECH and ESOP. However, the MCI continued to object to further privatization and the government's hands-off policy with respect to POSCO.[3] While the difference of policy objectives between the ministries and POSCO's management persisted so that the actual sell-off did not materialize during Kim Young-sam's presidency, POSCO did succeed in becoming listed on the New York Stock Exchange (NYSE) in October 1994 and the London Stock Exchange (LSE) in October 1995.

---

[2] One interesting episode regarding Chairman Park's intention to eliminate government interference as much as possible occurred when Park Tae-joon ordered his staff to come up with a proposal that would reduce the government share to 5% by selling off the shares to Pohang Institute of Technology (POSTECH) and ESOP in 1990. For the details of this episode, see the page 506 in Rhyu (1996).

[3] For example, Park Woon-Seo, then deputy minister of the MCI, said "privatization for efficiency gain does not apply to the case of POSCO, because POSCO as an SOE under government control has been supplying high quality steel products at lower prices." (Requoted from Rhyu 1996, originally from *Maeil Economic News*, March 23, 1995).

In July 1998, the Kim Dae-jung government resumed POSCO's privatization program. This implementation plan followed the guidance of the basic principles of the privatization program outlined in the past and shared the same basic principles as had been proposed by the MOF under the Kim Young-sam government. The Korean government decided to sell off the remaining shares owned by the government and the Korea Development Bank with the restriction that no single entity could own more than 3% of the total outstanding stocks. The Korean government favored a policy of a dispersed ownership structure with a professional management system, rather than management and control by a major controlling shareholder. The Ministry of Industry and Energy of Korea, which was the name of the newly reorganized MCI, could not block the privatization this time because of the government's desperate need to attract foreign investment to save the economy from the financial crisis. Furthermore, the market-oriented reform principle of the Kim Dae-jung government clashed with any lingering arguments to sustain government control of SOEs. According to the Ministry of Planning and Budget's (MPB) privatization plan on July 3, 1998, the government sold 3.14% that it owned and 2.73% owned by the Korea Development Bank to foreign buyers in the form of Depository Receipts (DR) in December 1998, and 8% owned by the Korea Development Bank again in the form of DR in July 1999. In preparation for the post-privatization period, POSCO introduced the "Global Professional Management" system based on recommendations from the consultancy group McKinsey in 1999. POSCO also purchased 3% of the total outstanding shares from the Korea Development Bank in December 1999 and June 2000.

Before the final sale of its remaining shares, the Korean government carried out various preparation measures for POSCO to successfully privatize. In September 2000, the government formally established a professional management system with a strong board of directors through a revision of POSCO's articles of incorporation. They also nullified the 3% ceiling limit of ownership to help induce more effective pressure on POSCO's professional management from financial markets. POSCO actually completed its privatization project in October 2000 by selling off the 4.6% owned by the Korea Development Bank to foreign markets in the form of DRs, and 2.24% owned by the Korea Development Bank to POSCO in the form of treasury stock.

Despite a decades-long tradition of self-autonomy by the professional management teams of POSCO, the Korean government sometimes failed to resist the temptations of seeking to exercise "control". Early in 2002, for example, the Korean government tried to interfere by pressuring then CEO and chairman, Yoo Sang-Boo, to resign, even though most shareholders, particularly foreign institutional investors, generally supported Yoo's renewal for another term as CEO and chairman of the board. In some sense, Yoo himself was the source of trouble because he was implicated in possible wrongdoings for his own personal benefit. First, without disclosing it to the board of directors, he donated several hundreds of millions of U.S. dollars of POSCO money to POSTECH and its foundation so that they could purchase POSCO stocks. Second, he ordered the company to retain its SK Telecom shares, even though this led to financial losses for the company, solely to maintain a friendly relationship based on cross-shareholding between the two companies. Yoo allegedly made these decisions to support the renewal of his term as chairman. Third, the prosecutor's office's investigation of Yoo's possible embezzlement to help his personal connection with political circles finally moved the government to exercise its influence in the CEO and chairman selection process to remove him. Foreign institutional investors, however, did not appreciate the government interference because it conflicted with the promotion of fair and competitive markets with economic freedom and strong protection of private property ownership (*Donga Daily*, July 13, 2003).[4]

Yoo's case damaged POSCO's image with respect to its corporate governance practices. Even though POSCO had been praised for excellent performance in the global market, it could not be free itself from the criticism that the current corporate governance structure overprotected management, leaving too much discretion to the CEO, i.e., the "management entrenchment" problem (Shliefer and Vishny 1989). Faced with this criticism about management entrenchment and a lower price-earnings ratio and dividends compared with international competitors, Lee Ku-Taek was chosen to succeed as CEO and chairman. Lee strived to raise the corporate governance structure of POSCO up to the highest global standards. The Korean government's experience with POSCO greatly influenced how it chose to later privatize KT (Rhyu and Kim 2009, 153–159).

However, in 2009, after the Lee Myung-bak government took office, CEO Lee Ku-Taek withdrew from his position due to political pressure, despite having a high managerial performance record and 1 year left in his term. There were debates and interpretations about the process of Lee Ku-Taek withdrawing in the middle of his term and CEO Chung Joon-yang being appointed. President Lee Myung-bak's elder brother, National Assembly Member Lee Sang-deuk and politically influential Vice Minister of Ministry of Knowledge and Economy, Park Young-joon, intervened in the CEO appointment process, and through the newly appointed CEO, their political power intervened in a lot of rights and interests. It is a widely accepted theory that this led to the current management aggravation. Park Young-joon exerted various pressures, such as declaring "the next term is Chung Joon-yang" at a meeting with Lee Ku-Taek, before the opening of the POSCO CEO recommendation committee.

The newly appointed CEO Chung Joon-yang expanded 41 subsidiary companies during his 5 years in office with excessive expansion management, and 18 of these are already in an impaired capital situation. It was also revealed that POSCO took over two places related to Lee Sang-deuk, which exponentially increased the market price damage to POSCO, and the prosecution is undertaking an investigation regard-

[4] Foreign institutional investors welcomed the renewal of Yoo's term as CEO and chairman because of his excellent performance despite the implications and indictment. They did not appreciate the Korean government's interference requesting them to object to Yoo. The author's confirmed the negative responses of foreign institutional investors against the government's intervention through an anonymous interview with a CEO in charge of Investors Relations of a large Korean company who maintains a close relationship with foreign institutional investors.

ing this (*Newsis*, October 5, 2015). The prosecution and the media is saying that President Lee Myung-bak's close aides have been personalizing POSCO for 5 years. Recently, coinciding with recession in the global steel market, POSCO recorded a 96 billion KRW net loss during the term, on the 2015 consolidated fiscal year basis. It is the first time in 47 years that POSCO recorded an annual loss. POSCO's 2015 sales (58.192 trillion KRW) and operating profit (2.41 trillion KRW) each decreased 10.6% and 25%.

After privatization, the government no longer holds a single share of POSCO, but it is questionable how the newly elected President's close aides elected POSCO's chief executive, and engaged in predatory rent-seeking. Considering the advanced corporate governance structure POSCO achieved after privatization, such a reality is difficult to imagine. POSCO introduced the outside director system (seven outside directors, five inside directors), and the independence of the board of directors was strengthened with the separation of the CEO and the chairman of the board of directors. To elect a more transparent and independent CEO, after February 2006, the articles of company were revised to employ a CEO candidate recommendation committee. In addition, five professional committees centering on outside directors were invigorated, implementing a more efficient decision making process.

On top of this, there is an independent audit committee entirely composed of being outside directors, and an autonomous external auditor is also appointed. Furthermore, various systems to protect the rights of minority shareholders such as proxy voting and a cumulative voting system were introduced. From the perspective of formal institutions, POSCO's corporate governance structure is without a doubt advanced. *Financial Asia* (April 2010) selected POSCO as South Korea's No.1 management company, and World Steel Dynamics (April 2010) chose POSCO as the No.1 competitive steel company in the world. Ever since 2004, Korea Corporate Governance Service has selected POSCO as the best corporate governance structure company for years. Also, in August 2002, United Kingdom's *Euro Money* ranked POSCO second in transparency and corporate governance structure among 650 large conglomerates in emerging markets. *Fortune* (in 2003 and 2005) selected POSCO as the No.1 World's Most Admired Company in the steel sector, and *Forbes* (in 2002 and 2003) selected POSCO as the No.1 World's Most Efficient Company in the steel industry.

However, following privatization, advancement in corporate governance structure did not properly operate within POSCO's management. How can we explain such a reality? First, we can see the limitations of ownership structure. In 2002, the POSTECH foundation purchased KDB's share, and with 3.34% of POSCO's entire share, became its largest shareholder. The largest shareholder in 2014 was the National Pension Service (3.54%), in 2005 SK Telecom (2.85%), in 2006 the National Pension Service (2.86%), in 2007 Nippon Steel Corporation (5.04%), and since 2008 the National Pension Service has continually been the largest shareholder, owning close to 6% of its shares. In December 2015, National Pension Service's fund amounted to 51.2 trillion KRW, and 32.2% of this is invested in the stock market, making it the largest institutional investor in South Korea.

However, there have been ongoing criticisms regarding the management professionalism and independence of the National Pension Service. There are clear limitations on the corporate governance structure of the National Pension Service. The chairman of the board of the National Pension Service is recommended by the Minister of Health and Welfare, and appointed by the President. The auditor of the National Pension Service is also recommended by the Minister of Strategy and Finance and appointed by the President. In actuality, the structure of the National Pension Service is dominated by the President and the government, so it is hard to expect independence and professionalism. In the meantime, there were many cases where the South Korean government mobilized the National Pension Service for political purposes. Compared to the pensions of advanced countries, the investment return rate was not high, so ultimately, it was criticized as having caused damage to the subscribers and the people. So, the newly elected President was able to become directly involved in the decision making of National Pension Service, and it was easy for the President to interfere in POSCO's management through its largest shareholder, the National Pension Service.

There were times when SK Telecom and Nippon steel were the largest shareholders, but they did not dominate management, or have large enough shares to directly oppose government intervention. Their purpose was to maintain long-term strategic alliance relations without the intention of dominating management control. In the same vein, the share ownership of foreign investors amounted to 69.25% in 2004, and 52.94% in 2014, yet they were all dispersed investors. Thus, they did not show much interest in monitoring management, and only pursued short-term capital gain. For example, since 2007, Warren Buffett's Berkshire Hathaway owned approximately 4.5% of POSCO's shares. After gaining considerable capital profits, in early 2014, all shares were sold. Under such conditions, POSCO is vulnerable to so-called managerial entrenchment, and was easy to become the target of a political authority's predatory rent-seeking.

Meanwhile, POSCO introduced the outside director system in 1997, and from 1997 to 1999, the proportion of parachute appointment personnel among the outside directors exceeded 60%. The proportion of POSCO's parachute appointments was sustained at 50% until 2002, and continuously decreased to one person from 2004 to 2015. So, then, the outside director system was able to function properly. However, as noted in the reality of government intervention under the Lee Myung-bak administration, in actuality, the outside director system has failed to protect POSCO from direct political intervention from the government, which is a major shareholder, and from predatory rent-seeking.

The management failure case of privatized POSCO raises interesting questions regarding the relationship between privatized companies and politics in the period of democratization. POSCO is an exceptional case which succeeded under the special political ties of President Park Chung-hee and CEO Park Tae-jun during the authoritarian period. At the time, an advanced corporate governance structure of related economic institutions had not been established, but the developmental state, marked by a drive to modernize and industrialize South Korea, and the politics of the developmental dictatorship were responsible for POSCO's success (Rhyu and

Lew 2013). POSCO was a public enterprise, but did not generate agency costs, and was protected by absolute power but not connected to corruption. Rather than well-designed institutions, it was the unique corporate culture, nationalistic tenacity, and the entrepreneurship of Park Chung-hee and Park Tae-joon which made POSCO's success possible.

Political pressure on POSCO started after the inauguration of the first civilian President, Kim Young-sam. As a political retaliation against CEO Park Tae-joon, who emerged as political competition in the presidential election process, President Kim Young-sam eliminated CEO Park Tae-joon's influence on POSCO, and instead appointed the politically close CEO Kim Man-jae. Paradoxically, after democratization and in a democratic government, POSCO's autonomy was destroyed and direct political intervention and rent-seeking began. At least in the case of POSCO, it was a trigger for repeated failure in politics where democratization impeded POSCO's autonomous management and transparency, and corruption and inefficiency increased. Until recently, such a paradox in democratization has been ongoing in the case of privatized POSCO.

3.4 KT: Limits to Formal Institutions and Repetitive Rent-Seeking

While POSCO's privatization processes revealed the dynamic power between the various government ministries and POSCO's management, KT's privatization process exposed the actual orbit of policy responses to the rapidly changing regulatory and competitive environment of the telecommunications industry (Rhyu 1996). In other words, KT's privatization was the manifestation of a major policy option to effectively cope with the changing regulatory and competitive environments caused by frequent technological breakthroughs.

In 1987, KT first attempted privatization with the goal of incorporating the company through a sale of 49% of the total outstanding shares to the market. This plan failed to materialize mainly because the local market lacked the capacity to absorb such a large offering. In 1990, a similar privatization plan was attempted, with the goals of selling 49% to the market through ESOP and a public offering in the following year. Again, due to the limited liquidity of the capital market, the government decided to postpone the plan until 1996. In 1993, KT's privatization plan finally proceeded in earnest under the Kim Young-sam government. According to the plan at that time, 49% of the total outstanding stocks would be sold off through in several phases until 1996.

The basic motives behind the privatization program included the following: (1) to enhance the company's competitiveness in preparation for market opening and deregulation that would change its near monopoly status into a more competitive market environment; (2) to radically innovate KT to achieve efficiency gains; and (3) to establish a professional management system with a dispersed ownership structure (modeled after POSCO's impressive performance under autonomous professional management). While the initial sale started in 1994, the actual sale of government-owned shares amounted to only 28.8% by 1996, mainly due to the sluggish state of the stock market and resistance by employees who feared for their job security.

The Kim Dae-jung government formulated and executed the final stage of KT's privatization. As with POSCO, in July 1998, the government classified KT's privatization as extremely urgent. KT thus attempted to formulate its privatization plan according to the guidelines of the government. However, the Ministry of Finance and Economy, the Ministry of Communication and Information, and the Ministry of Planning and Budget each announced separate plans concerning the details of KT's privatization strategy. This demonstrated the need for consultation and unified policy objectives within the government to facilitate the privatization. According to the plan, the main features of management innovation and privatization involved the following: (1) to restructure KT into a more efficient organization by divesting unprofitable business lines and business units/branches through voluntary retirement programs for existing employees by the year 2000; (2) to list KT on the Korean Stock Exchange by the end of the year; and (3) to promote DR issuance in foreign markets and strategic alliances with foreign telecommunication service providers in early 1999 to become a globally competitive telecommunications service company (MPB 1998).

The Korean government's privatization policy emphasized the critical role of foreign investors and KT's possible strategic alliances with global players. Through these international contributions, the Korean government sought to achieve two policy objectives: (1) to effectively cope with international pressure concerning the opening and deregulations of the telecommunications service market of Korea, and (2) to achieve fast and smooth privatization.

As explained above, the Korean government restructured the telecommunications service industry into a more open and free market by allowing competition in certain service sectors in the late 1980s and early 1990s. They sought to effectively confront the rapidly changing regulatory and competitive environments. The government hoped to transform KT into a more efficient and productive organization through management innovation and privatization, while allowing new regulations to gradually transform the industry from a closed exclusive monopoly into a more open and competitive entity.

Although privatization was viewed as an effective policy response to the rapidly changing regulatory and competitive environments in the telecommunications industry, KT's privatization languished. The urgency after the financial crisis, however, forced all of the related parties, including the labor unions, to agree to a fundamental restructuring through an expeditious and complete privatization. To accelerate the privatization process, the Korean government revised the relevant laws and regulations to create an environment more conducive to foreign investment and business alliances. For the corporate governance structure of the privatized KT, policymakers opted to establish a professional management team in charge of operations overseen by a strong and independent board of directors. They also sought to establish an effective protection mechanism against a possible hostile takeover after privatization. The government stipulated that the total amount of shares owned by foreigners could not exceed 49% of the total outstanding shares, and no foreign person is allowed to become a major shareholder with the clear goal of a dispersed ownership structure for KT after privatization.

The government's strong commitment brought remarkable results. First, the Korean government succeeded in selling 14.4% of the total outstanding shares it had owned in the form of DR in May 1999, and 17.8% in the form of DRs in June 2001. In January 2002, Microsoft decided to establish a strategic alliance with KT by acquiring 3% of KT's equity for $500 million. KT completed its privatization in the summer of 2002 when the government sold 11.8% of its total outstanding shares in the form of Exchangeable Bonds (EB) and Bonds with Warrants (BW), and 28.4% of the total outstanding shares to domestic investors (Rhyu and Kim 2009, 159–162).

With complete privatization, KT reformed its corporate governance structure. To improve the independence of the board of directors, it organized the board of directors to center on outside directors (in 2015 the percentage of outside director was 73%), and the roles of CEO and chairman of the board of directors were separated. The audit committee, evaluation committee, and compensation committee were all composed of outside directors. An outside director was elected through an outside director candidate recommendation committee, and they were granted the authority to evaluate the management performance of the CEO, and propose to terminate. A cumulative voting system was introduced to protect shareholder value, and from March 2003, general meetings of stockholders were broadcast live on the Internet.

In addition, the compensation of the CEO was interlocked with the stock price. Candidates for CEO were decided through the CEO recommendation committee with outsiders as key personnel, and responsibility for management of professional entrepreneurs was strengthened by annually signing a management contract with the newly elected CEO. Furthermore, with the introduction of a written voting and proxy voting system, the authority of minority shareholders was strengthened. Such introduction of an advanced corporate governance structure was sufficient to receive high praise from both home and abroad. In September 2015, KT received an grade of A+ for five consecutive years in the corporate governance sector supervised by the Korea Corporate Governance Service, receiving high praise for its professional and independent composition of the board of directors, active operation of the board of directors, protection of shareholders' rights, transparent disclosure system, and operation of impartial audit institution. In September 2003, *Economy* selected KT as a top company in emerging market corporate structures. It received an all-around excellent evaluation for its financial structure, financial transparency, and operation of the board of directors, shareholder relations, and interest relations of management. In September 2002, Goldman Sachs chose KT as the best practice in Asia's corporate structure, and S&P selected KT as the most transparent local company among 100 companies in the Asia Pacific. Like POSCO, the economic reforms and advanced corporate governance structures promoted by KT sufficiently complied with global standards, at least in form.

However, contrary to its appearance of having an advanced corporate governance structure, after privatization, there were many instances where the new political authorities directly and repeatedly intervened in management. The new administration regarded KT as a trophy for winning the elections, and the practice of appointing the president's close aides as CEO or major executive became a custom. In March 2009, during the Lee Myung-bak administration, Lee Suk-chae, who worked as the Chief of Economy during the Kim Young-sam administration, was appointed president of KT. Lee Suk-chae, who was a member of the National Economic Advisory Council of the Lee Myung-bak administration, was close to President Lee. The media revealed that the background of Lee Suk-chae's appointment was political, as he was even recommended by President Kim Young-sam's group, which played a big role in the appearance of President Lee Myung-bak. President Lee Suk-chae, who was reappointed for a 3-year term in March 2012, was pressured to resign under the Park Geun-hye administration, despite the fact that his term was slated to last until March 2015.

In February and October of 2013, the People's Solidarity for Participatory Democracy (PSPD) brought accusations against Lee Suk-chae to the prosecution for work malpractices, and the prosecution's investigation accelerated. According to PSPD's submission of the bill of indictment, CEO Lee was involved in businesses such as "SmartADmall" "OIC Language Visual," and "CyberMBA," damaging the companies' profits. With this reinforcement of the prosecution's investigation, CEO Lee Suk-chae resigned his position of CEO at KT on November 12, 2013. On January 27, 2014, Hwang Chang-gyu, former president of Samsung Electronics, took office, and the investigation on Lee Suk-chae remains in progress. The resignation of former CEO Lee Suk-chae was not an outcome based on KT's corporate governance structure. Major personnel appointed by the former government were replaced with personnel chosen by the new political leadership, and the PSPD's accusation and prosecutor's investigation could be interpreted as a good justification for such.

How could the government possibly pursue predatory rent-seeking towards KT despite intensification of the global communications market and heightened pressure for technological innovation? From a formal institution's point of view, although an advanced corporate governance structure had been established, in actual management, why couldn't such formal institutions operate at all? Factors such as the limitations of an ownership structure without the presence of a private majority shareholder, managerial entrenchment being a blind spot of management, direct intervention by political authorities, and side effects of parachute appointment may be explanatory. In 2013, National Pension Service, which was dominated by the government, owned 7.64% as the largest shareholder, Mirae Asset Global Investments held 4.52% as the second largest shareholder, employee ownership comprised 1.2% of ownership, and foreign-owned shares comprised 46%. As in the case of POSCO, the foreign shareholders were dispersed, and with capital profit gain as its purpose, they remained indifferent towards management monitoring.

Thc argument that managerial transparency is higher with a higher proportion of foreign share ownership does not apply, at least in the cases of POSCO and KT. The

National Pension Service is the largest institutional investor and has a crucial weakness in its corporate governance structure. Furthermore, in the National Pension Service Fund Operation Guidelines, even in the case of the National Pension Service being the largest shareholder or a major shareholder, there are no guidelines regarding actively exercising voting rights such as calling for a meeting of the board of directors, appointing a CEO, or introducing agendas.

Since both the chairman of the board and auditors are appointed by the president, management is completely subordinate to political power. In addition, there is a high possibility for the president and the ruling party to abuse and misuse KT for their political interests. However, institutions to monitor such abuses are weak. In the current political structure of South Korea, political or social monitoring by the opposition party or the media, or the monitoring system within the pension system, are not effective.

Such limitations in ownership structure have been the institutional origin of negative effects such as management abuse by the management and political intervention, and widespread recruitment of parachute appointment personnel. Such a phenomenon has been revealed even in the appointment process of former CEO Lee Suk-chae. In 2009, CEO Lee Suk-chae was not qualified to become the president of KT. It was against Article 25 of the KT Articles of Association, which states that "personnel who was an executive at a competing company within the past 2 years cannot become the CEO of KT". CEO Lee was an outside director of SK C&C, a rival company of KT. However, with political pressure from the newly inaugurated Lee Myung-bak administration, in November 2008, KT held a general shareholders' meeting to revise the article. The article was changed to allow the CEO to have prior experience as an executive at a rival company within the last 2 years. This was criticized as an 'article revision for Lee Suk-chae'. At the time, some in the media brought up the suspicion that the Lee Myung-bak administration intervened in KT's article revision.

After this, CEO Lee Suk-chae, who was appointed and supported by Lee Myung-bak administration, revised the Articles of Association twice. In March 2010, the article excluding civilian committee members (one person) and former presidents (one person) from participating in the CEO recommendation committee to block the possibility of external intervention in the process of appointing the chairman was revised. In the revised Article of Association, the CEO recommendation committee is to be composed of only one inside board of director, and outside directors. Also in March of 2013, the article was revised to allow executives that have work experience at rival companies or subsidiary companies to be appointed as outside directors, and the term of outside directors was extended to a maximum of 10 years from a 3-year term, which could be repeated once. The labor union and civil society argued that this revision of the article was a part of a 'Lee Suk-chae reappointment project'.

After this article revision, Lee Suk-chae recruited people he had personal ties as outside directors. The board of directors Lee Suk-chae appointed in 2013 was composed of four inside directors and seven outside directors, and most had personal ties with CEO Lee Suk-chae or were directly connected with the Lee Myung-bak administration. For example, inside director Pyo Hyun-myung and outside director Kim Eung-hwan are CEO Lee Suk-chae's high school alumni. Outside director Lee Chun-ho is President Lee Myung-bak's presidential campaign personnel, and inside director Song Do-Kyun has been revealed as being selected due to his acquaintance with President Lee's elder brother Lee Sang-deuk. Outside director Park Byung-won, a former economic bureaucrat, was personally close to CEO Lee Suk-chae when he was the chief economist during the Kim Young-sam administration. Outside director Song Jong-hwan, former chief of the Central Intelligence Agency, participated in President Park Geun-hye's think tank.

Meanwhile, CEO Lee Suk-chae recruited many parachute appointed personnel at major positions at KT from the political world. Executive director Kim Eun-hye, the chief of KT Communications in 2013, was the spokesperson for the Blue House during the Lee Myung-bak administration, and Oh Se-Hyeon, chief of the headquarters of KT, publically supported candidate Lee Myung-bak during the 17th presidential elections. Kim Gyu-seong, president of KT Mhows, was formerly a member of the standing advisory committee of President Lee Myung-bak government transition committee, and Huh Jeung-soo, who acted as an outside director from 2009, was formerly on Lee Myung-bak's transition committee. Lee Tae-gyu, who was an executive director at KT Economy and Management Research Lab, used to be the secretary to the President for Speechwriting and Documentation for President Lee Myung-bak.

The proportion of KT parachute appointments did not change much before and after democratization. After government monopolization disappeared, a structure was formed that allowed for the possibility of the mismanagement of management. The spike of increased parachute appointments that are due to personal connections with the CEO rather than parachute appointment of politicians or former bureaucrats can be examined. In addition, CEO Lee Suk-chae made KT purchase troubled companies with ties to his relatives at a high price, which led to the accusation of having resulted in large losses for KT and is currently under investigation. Regardless of the results of the investigation in progress, in the absence of an owner and with negligent monitoring, the structure where the CEO can pursue his own interests and damage the company in management continues. In the case of the third quarter of 2013, among the three major mobile carriers in South Korea, KT's profit rate decreased to −7.3%, a stark contrast to SKT and LGU+, both of which recorded a 1–2% growth rate in profits.

The changes in managerial recruitment of POSCO is a typical example of managerial entrenchment that can frequently occur in a newly privatized company without an owner. It is also a case representative of a neutralized formal institution where the informal network displays more power. Neutralized corporate governance structure and political intervention combined to lead KT to fall into a trap of greater corruption and inefficiency. KT is a meaningful case which shows the limitations of corporate governance structures and the negative impacts of informal networks in South Korean privatized companies.

3.5 The Korea Development Bank: Return of Developmental State and Reversal of Privatization

KDB, which was established as a public enterprise in April 1954, was a necessary core financial institution for South Korea to pursue its developmental state. It was a crucial channel of policy loans, treasury loans, and investments that intensively invested its limited financial capital in strategic industries. Immediately after the Korean War, KDB's core project was economic reconstruction, and after the 1960s its major projects were providing export financing for companies, facilities financing, and inviting foreign capital to invest in heavy and chemical industrialization. At the time, KDB was an essential organization in South Korea that promoted government-led export oriented industrialization in poor conditions with undeveloped financial and capital markets.

Regardless of this positive role, KDB was unsuccessful in actively coping with changes in domestic and international financial markets. So, it was under a significant amount of pressure to advance its business areas and reform. The 1997 Asian financial crisis in South Korea highlighted the vulnerability of the financial industry and management failure of *chaebols*. KDB was not free from these two criticisms. KDB was an axis of bureaucratic finance, which was indicated as the source of the opaqueness and inefficiency of the South Korean financial industry. The South Korean government and private enterprises depended on indirect financing to procure investment capital for industrialization through banks rather than the stock market. Financial bureaucrats and politicians were able to arbitrarily exercise regulatory power in the finance market for a long time. Moreover, there were no other incentives for the developmental state and bureaucrats to develop the stock market, and they did not hold specific policy or vision to do so. With this, the competitiveness of South Korea's capital market was vulnerable. Direct intervention of the government in the finance market and banks was specified through intervention in personnel matters in arbitrary monetary policy and banks. As a result, banks did not have the motivation to evaluate business value and evaluate the likelihood of their loans being repaid, nor could they develop the capability to do so. This ensured that South Korean banks would be left behind in international competitiveness.

Right after the economic crisis, the South Korean government examined the financial health of banking institutions with the help of the IMF and the World Bank. Intensive reform was carried out as a result. As seen in Table 3.1, a total of 600 financial institutions closed. Among 1200 financial institutions, from 1997 to 2002, 467 were thrown out of the market, and 153 of those remaining were forced to merge with other healthy financial institutions.

Furthermore, the corporate governance structures of major banks in the market were reformed to reflect the same structure that non-financial companies held. Various systems to strengthen the rights of consumers and minority shareholders were introduced. These include improvements in the independence of the board of directors, separation of the role of CEO from that of the chairman of the board of directors, and the strengthening of accountability of the largest shareholder. In

Table 3.1 Closures and mergers of financial institutions in South Korea (1997–2002)

	Number of institutions as of the end of 1997	Restructured		Newly established	Number of institutions as of the end of March 2002
		Exited	Merged		
Banks	33	5	9	1	20
Securities	36	6	2	16	44
Insurance	50	9	6	9	44
Others[a]	1982	447	136	32	1431
Total	2101	467	153	58	1539

Source: Financial Supervisory Service (FSS)
[a]Merchant Banks, Investment Trust Funds, Mutual Funds, Credit Unions, Lease companies, etc.

Table 3.2 Equity participation in domestic banks by foreign nationals after the economic crisis

	1997		2000	
Bank	Weight of shareholding by foreign nationals	Major shareholders	Weight of shareholding by foreign nationals	Major shareholders
Korea Housing and Commercial	41.2	Government (22.4%)	65.4	Bank of New York (13.1%) ING Group (10%)
Kookmin	37.0	Government (15.2%) Bank of New York (8.4%)	58.2	Goldman Sachs (11.1%)
Korea First	0.1	Korea Life Insurance (4.9%)	Over 51.0	New Bridge Capital (51%)
Shinhan	23.4	Korean residents in Japan (42.9%)	48.9	Korean residents in Japan (27%)
KorAm	29.4	BOA (18.6%)	61.5	Carlyle Consortium (40.1%) BOA (10.1%)
Korea exchange	2.7	BOA (47.9%)	26.4	Commerz Bank (31.6%)
Hana	21.3	Kyobo Life Insurance (7.7%)	20.3	Allianz Group (12.5%) IFC (International Finance Corporation (2.8%)

Source: Samsung Economic Research Institute (2001)

particular, as in Table 3.2, foreign nationals became the largest shareholder of major banks in the market, and they started to manage the banks according to international standards and market principles. This shows that the custom of government-controlled credit allocation, where the bank used to be controlled by the government, came to an end. Such reform in corporate governance structures is seen as having positively influenced the improvement of the earnings rate of South Korean financial institutions, as well as international competitiveness.

Meanwhile, KDB played a big role in the process of restructuring. Since the Kim Dae-jung administration simultaneously implemented financial and business reform, bank restructuring was impossible if KDB did not issue restructuring bonds to insolvent enterprises. Even after overcoming the economic crisis, the South Korean government introduced a quick underwriting scheme in January 2001 to maintain the stability of the bond market and the real economy. In a sense, it is an extended version of the existing primary collateralized bond obligation (CBO) scheme, whereby government-backed guarantee support is provided for newly issued sub-investment grade bonds. Developing the market for CBOs has been a policy priority since the Daewoo crisis of 1999, as the market can pool risks and enhance bond market access for companies across the risk spectrum. Based on this institution, KDB was able to buy up 20 trillion won (about 16 billion USD) worth of insolvent bonds. In this way, it cannot be denied that KDB contributed to the restructuring of South Korean financial institutions and *chaebol* companies from 1997 to the present.

However, despite this success, KDB became the last bastion of government-led restructuring, and remained a government-owned financial institution where government-controlled credit allocation continued. During the restructuring processes, which were begun during the 1997 financial crisis and again during the 2008 global economic crisis, KDB, a national bank representative of Korea, became a dinosaur enterprise with a total of 130 insolvent subsidiary companies (377 if including all subsidiary companies such as funds) in September 2015, including 18 companies to be restructured such as Daewoo Shipbuilding & Marine Engineering, Daewoo E&C, KDB Life Insurance, Dongbu Steel, and STX. It also includes 10 financial subsidiary companies and 102 investment companies. With this, in September 2015, KDB's insolvent bonds are increasing, having already reached 3.1 trillion won, or 2.58%. In 2015, KDB recorded 1.9 trillion won in net losses. The procedure to clear insolvent bonds and reform insolvent subsidiary companies and resell is in progress, but the results have not been good. These losses and the accumulation of insolvent bonds of KDB remain a burden on the taxpayers, and on the South Korean economy as a whole. By becoming a sponsor of so-called zombie companies rejected by general commercial banks, the size of KDB's insolvent companies increased, and there were allegations that South Korea's entire economy has entered a crisis.

For a long time, there have been many debates on how to solve KDB's accumulated insolvent bonds after the 1997 economic crisis and how to adjust KDB's core business in the future. This is also a part of the strategic argument on how to strengthen the South Korean financial industry's international competitiveness against the endless competition of the global financial market and the strong trend towards globalization. Lee Myung-bak, the ruling party's candidate during the presidential elections on December 13, 2007, said that South Korea should "privatize KDB in order to prepare capital to support small and medium-sized companies," which was the first public announcement regarding KDB's privatization.

He proposed to separate the bank by selling the investment bank duties to the private sector through a merger and acquisition, developing a 'private investment bank', and proposed putting the 'downsized KDB' in charge of national bank tasks such as procuring long-term capital for industry sectors.

Based on this statement, the Lee Myung-bak government revised the Korea Development Bank Act on April 2009. Fifty-six years after the establishment of the KDB, Article 1 of the Korea Development Bank Act was changed to "regulate necessary factors to implement KDB's privatization process". Following this, in October 2009, the original KDB was separated into three companies including KDB, KDB Holding Company, and Korea Finance Corporation. The privatization process of the downsized KDB was accelerated. The Lee Myung-bak government privatization of KDB was a part of a strategy to make KDB into a globally competitive large-size investment bank and foster South Korea into becoming Northeast Asia's financial hub.

To promote KDB's transformation into investment bank, in the summer of 2008, the Lee Myung-bak government proposed investing 6 billion dollars in Lehman Brothers, and during the negotiation process, Lehman Brothers declared bankruptcy on September 15th, 2008. At that time, it was confirmed that core personnel, including then President Lee Myung-bak, Minister of Strategy and Finance Kang Man-soo, and Chairman of the Financial Supervisory Commission Jeon Kwang-Woo had strongly supported this project (Park 2012). At that time, the president of KDB was Min Euoo-sung, who supported President Lee Myung-bak's campaign and was acting head of the Lehman Brothers Seoul office immediately before the incident. Plans to privatize KDB did not make much progress with the 2008 financial crisis and 2010 euro crisis.

The newly inaugurated Park Geun-hye administration suspended the privatization process of KDB, and decided that the institution should revert back to its original policy finance-centered form. In May 2014, the Park Geun-hye administration revised Article 1 of the Korea Development Bank Act again, to re-write KDB's objective as "develop and promote industries, expand infrastructure […] supply and manage sustainable acceleration of growth". Following this, in January 2015, the three organizations that KDB had been divided into were integrated and re-launched as an 'integrated KDB'. It meant that KDB's privatization had officially ceased, and although it did perform the functions of commercial finance, the institution would revert back to center on policy finance. At a chief secretary meeting on July 22, 2013, president Park Geun-hye stated that "in the meantime there were criticisms that because the function of policy finance is dispersed among many different organizations and is duplicated, it reduces efficiency and lacks risk management, so we are at a point to reform the policy finance system", a statement which served as a pre-notification of the intended halt in the debate over KDB's privatization.

The 'strengthening the role of IBK (Industrial Bank of Korea) and KDB' measures suggested by the Financial Services Commission on November 1, 2015 were interpreted as an action telling government-owned KDB and IBK not to compete with the private financial market and to be loyal to their intrinsic duties as national banks. At the inauguration ceremony in January 2015, Hong Ki-taek, the CEO of the integrated KDB, emphasized that "this year, the role of risk taker will be more boldly pushed in areas difficult for the private sector to participate in."

President Park Geun-hye's decision to suspend the privatization illustrated not only the financial and administrative waste in expenses used for the 5 years of pushing for privatization, but also the opposition from the international community. In the "2015 National Trade Estimate Report on Foreign Trade Barriers" made public in April 2, 2015 by the United States Trade Representative (USTR) expressed discontent stating that "Under the amended KDB Act, which became effective as of January 1, 2015, the public policy financing role of the KDB is to be strengthened and the KDB will continue its traditional role of providing public policy financial support to Korean industry and companies. The U.S. Government has concerns regarding Korea's decision to reverse the plan to privatize the KDB, and will continue to monitor the lending policies of the KDB and other government-owned or affiliated financial institutions (USTR 245)" (Froman 2015; Park 2015). Furthermore, by integrating the three organizations, Korea Development Bank's capital ratio by the standard of Bank for International Settlements dropped to about 12%, which created increased worries over asset soundness.

What then made Park Geun-hye suspend the privatization policy of KDB? And how should this be interpreted? President Park Geun-hye prefers the developmental state strategy, which her father President Park Chung-hee established. It appears that she holds a strong policy idea towards active intervention by the government and government-controlled credit allocation, and active support for large conglomerates. It is also true that she had a strong nostalgia for the developmental state period's policy decision making process and national strategy. In addition, in order to practice the so-called creative economy she promoted, it can be assumed that she felt the need for a strong policy finance institution. Feelings of and hostility and a desire to contain former President Lee Myung-bak, who is from the same Saenuri Party, and with whom she has a politically conflicting relationship, also played a partial role. As suspicion about corruption among Lee Myung-bak government's major personnel emerged as a social issue, not only with regards to KDB's privatization, but also in other economic policies, it seems to have also acted as a political intention to fundamentally block KDB's privatization pursued by the Lee Myung-bak administration.

Whatever the reason, suspension of KDB's privatization signifies a reconstruction of South Korea's developmental state, at least in the finance sector, even as it was weakening or dissolving after the Asian financial crisis. Under a structure where government-led policy is difficult to execute because most commercial banks became foreign-owned, if even KDB were to be privatized and transformed into an investment bank, it would be tantamount to the end of industrial policy to mobilize for corporate restructuring and investment. In a situation where the president herself preferred a developmental state-type policy idea, it was probably difficult to allow the privatization of KDB, which is the last bastion of industrial policy. Furthermore, in Park Geun-hye administration that demonstrated a self-righteous leadership style, it was probably difficult for the opinions of expert groups and relevant bureaucrats to be reflected in the final decision regarding the suspension of KDB's privatization.

Separate from president Park Geun-hye's policy preference, the suspension of KDB privatization also played out with the inertia of bureaucratic politics and the dominant coalition of an informal network centering on KDB for a long time. After the 1997 economic crisis, the proportion of parachute appointments among South Korea's major banks outside directors did not decrease much. In banks where foreign nationals are major shareholders, the proportion of parachute appointed personnel gradually increased from 7% in 1999 to 35% in 2012. In the case of national banks, where the government is a major shareholder, with extensive pressure for reform from right after the 1997 economic crisis until 2004, at the proportion of parachute appointments remained steady at 20–40%, but after 2005 it exceeded 50%, and as of 2012 it was 71%. This signifies that in the dimension of formal institutions and ownership structure, the share of foreign nationals is expanding in major banks, and corporate governance structure has improved, so government-controlled credit allocation weakened and the developmental state was in a stage of dissolving.

However, from the informal network side, indirect monitoring through parachute appointed personnel continues, and this shows that the developmental state has not completely disappeared. Parachute appointed personnel, who are the hidden fabric of the developmental state in the finance industry, are still maintained and are being reproduced. After inauguration, Park Geun-hye administration politically pressured Kang Man-soo, the president of KDB financial holding company who was appointed by president Lee Myung-bak, to step down despite having 3 years remaining in his term. After this, in April 2013, Hong Ki-taek, who served in president Park Geun-hye's election camp, was newly appointed as the CEO. CEO Lee Dong-gul, who was appointed as successor of Hong Ki-taek in February 2016, also had a similar background. The labor union of the KDB expressed criticism by stating that "the Financial Service Commission's recommendation of appointee Lee is a favor returned in exchange for his election support in the 2012 presidential election" (Kim 2013).

Looking at the composition of KDB's outside directors in 2013, excluding the inside board of directors, the majority were personnel who directly participated in president Park Geun-hye's election campaign. They were personnel who were affiliated with the think-tank for then presidential candidate Park Geun-hye, the Institute for the Future of the State, who individually supported the election campaign, or who served at the Blue House. There were also some people that had personal connections with the CEO. Among these people, many did not have knowledge or experience regarding KDB's work. President Park Geun-hye announced that she would appoint "people who share the government's philosophy" to major positions in government-affiliated organizations. The majority opinion holds that these outside directors cannot expect to have independence and professionalism and monitor the CEO, and make decisions regarding KDB's work. Moreover, when KDB's corporate governance structure reverted to that of a government bank with the suspension of privatization, it became a structure where the negative effect of informal networks was strengthened. The president of the bank is recommended by the Financial Services Commission and appointed by the president, and the chairman of the Financial Services Commission is appointed by the president. In 2013, the president of KDB and chairman of the board of directors were not separated, and the president of the bank holds concurrent positions as chairman of the risk management committee and the outside director candidate recommendation committee (*Money Today*, May 23, 2015).

Bureaucrats of related departments who exercised regulatory power towards KDB, together with high ranking employees of KDB, welcomed the suspension of privatization of KDB. Subsidiary companies that KDB owned were abused as a measure to maintain or cultivate this bank's organizational structure and personnel. According to Saenuri Party's lawmaker Oh Shin-hwan's government inspection records in 2015, all 43 retired employees from KDB were reemployed at KDB's subsidiary companies or loan companies. In addition, companies that received new loans and loan extensions 1 month before or after the transfer of one of KDB's former employees to their institution or post was to 37%, or 16 out of 43 companies (*Yonhap News*, September 12, 2015).

From the perspective of bureaucrats and KDB employees, if the restructuring of insolvent companies is delayed, and the number of subsidiary companies increases, the number of seats they can take also increases. Accordingly, the incident where KDB's privatization was suddenly suspended by President Park Geun-hye became an opportunity for the political world and bureaucrats to maintain their interests and the rights of the informal network, which they enjoyed in the past. This means the reconstruction of the distributive ruling coalition during the period of the developmental state in KDB.

3.6 Conclusion

Privatization requires a process of demolishing old institutions and building new ones. In Korea, privatization began for economic rationality, but the process involved political competition. There were fierce competition between the loser groups that would lose their vested interests with privatization and the winner group that would benefit from privatization. The cases of privatization may be an inevitable choice under the dual pressures of globalization and democratization. However, the path and outcome of privatization will vary according to the dynamics of domestic politics, which will be determined by who leads the political process of privatization and how. Moreover, the politics of privatization is not managed by existing formal institutions, but by informal networks.

Interesting facts were discovered through the three cases of privatization. Although the transfer of government shares to a majority private shareholder is important, as in the case of the NPS, it does not guarantee that it would generate meaningful outcomes. The NPS, which is not independent from the government and does not hold a transparent corporate governance structure, was not in a position to prevent government intervention and predatory rent-seeking. Presidents, politicians, and relevant bureaucrats could continue to pursue their political economic benefits through informal networks in the process of privatization. The managerial entrenchment of CEOs who were politically appointed in privatized companies amplified such negative effects. It was not easy to increase benefit for the people and establish transparent management. Such a phenomenon was not an exception in privatized companies with a high number of foreign shareholders.

Based on this research, several new questions have to be raised. First, the discussion on how much economic crises and the pressure of globalization can trigger and drive economic reforms such as privatization should be restarted. There were many cases where the achievement of privatization was incapacitated even in companies with very high percentage of foreign investor ownership in a period and in industry sectors under strong pressure from globalization. Second, more case studies should be done on the relation between formal institutions and informal networks in the privatization process, and their roles. Both in the case of KT, where the formal governance structure was well constructed, and in the case of KDB, where the corporate governance structure was not reformed, the reason the President's command was able to determine everything was because informal networks overrode formal institutions. Third, privatization could not become an opportunity for South Korea's developmental state to dissolve, and was misused as a chance for South Korea's developmental state to adapt to the new environment and reorganize. There are disputes on the dissolution of South Korea's developmental state, but before privatized companies in South Korea can operate properly, South Korea's developmental state cannot be said to have ended. Fourth, then, what is required for South Korea's developmental state to transform into a new development model suitable for globalization and democratization? The case of POSCO, where privatization under authoritarianism and the developmental state was more transparent, is enough to question the conventional wisdom of this question. However, the meaning of democracy is still accepted as the most important political foundation for a new development model. The continuous presentation of the need for democratic consolidation for South Korea's ongoing economic growth can be understood in the same context.

References

Barnett, Steven. 2000. Evidence on the Fiscal and Macroeconomic Impact of Privatization. Working Paper 130. International Monetary Fund (IMF), Washington, D.C., July.

Boycko, M., A. Shleifer, and R.W. Vishny. 1996. A Theory of Privatization. *The Economic Journal* 106 (435): 309–319.

Cook, P., and Y. Uchida. 2001. Privatization and Economic Growth in Developing Countries. Working Paper 7. Centre on Regulation and Competition, University of Manchester, Manchester, October.

Donga Daily. July 13, 2003.

D'Souza, J., W.C. Megginson, and R. Nash. 2001. Determinants of Performance Improvements in Privatized Firms: The Role of Restructuring and Corporate Governance. Social Science Research Network Working Paper Series, March.

Financial Supervisory Service (FSS) FSS. http://dart.Fss.or.kr/.

Froman, Michael B.G. 2015. National Trade Estimate Report on Foreign Trade Barriers. Washington D.C.: Office of the United States Trade Representative (USTR), March.

Frydman, R., C. Gray, M. Hessel, and A. Rapaczynski. 1999. When Does Privatization Work? The Impact of Private Ownership on Corporate Performance in the Transition Economies. *The Quarterly Journal of Economics* 4: 1154–1191.

Keohane, Robert O., and Helen V. Milner. 1996. *Internationalization and Domestic Politics*. Cambridge: Cambridge University.

Kim, Min-ha. 2013. Daetongnyong hanmadie… sanobunhaeng minyounghwa sashisang baekchi-hwa chungchaekkumyounggonsa sanobunhaeng tonghap kummulsal. [With the President's Comments… Privatization of KDB Virtually Rescinded, Urgent Integration of Korea Finance Corporation and KDB]. Mediaus. July 25. (in Korean).

Megginson, William L., and J.M. Netter. 2001. From State to Market: A Survey of Empirical Studies on Privatization. *Journal of Economic Literature* 2: 321–389.

Ministry of Planning and Budget of Korea. 1998. *Information on Management Innovation and Privatization Plan of KT*. December, www.mpb.go.kr.

———. 2002. *White Paper on Public Sector Reform,* December, Seoul Korea: Ministry of Planning and Budget of Korea.

Money Today. May 23, 2015.

Newsis. October 5, 2015.

North, Douglass C. 1990. *Institutions, Institutional Change and Economic Performance*. New York: Cambridge University Press.

Park, Sae-Yul. 2012. Lee Myungbak Kang Mansoo man-su, Lehman Brothers insu gangnyeok jiji-hatetda. [Lee Myung-bak and Kang Man-soo aggressively supported undertaking of Lehman Brothers', Korean American Journalist An Chi Yong, Disclosure of 'secret memo' by MB Economic Team] Pressian. (October 19). (in Korean).

Park, Soo-jin. 2015. Saneobeunhaeng chulbeomeun minyeonghwa pogittsaneop bojogeum buh-wal ruryeo. [Establishment of KDB is abandonment of Privatization…Concerns about Revival Industry Subsidies] Hankyung. (April 3). (in Korean).

Rhyu, Sang-Young. 1996. Privatization in Korea and Institutional Change: Comparison of POSCO and KT. In *Rethinking Korean Politics*, ed. Korean Political Science Association. Hanul Academy: Seoul.

Rhyu, Sang-young, and Seoungjoo Lee. 2006. Economic Reform and Changes in Informal Networks between Government and Business in South Korea. *The 21st Century Political Science Review* 16 (1): 46–68. (in Korean).

Rhyu, Sang-young, and Taekwon Kim. 2009. Corporate Governance Reform of Privatized Enterprises in Korea: A Comparative Study of POSCO and KT Cases. *Asian Corporate Governance Case Studies Series (Korea),* Hills Governance Center at Yonsei University.

Rhyu, Sang-young, and Seok-jin Lew. 2013. Pohang Iron & Steel Company. In *The Park Chung Hee Era: The Transformation of South Korea*, ed. Byung-Kook Kim and Ezra F. Vogel, 322–344. Cambridge: Harvard University Press.

Sachs, J., C. Zinnes, and Y. Eilat. 2000. The Gains from Privatization Economies: Is Change of Ownership Enough? *Discussion Paper 63. Consulting Assistance on Economic Reform (CAER) II, Harvard Institute for International Development,* Cambridge, MA.

Samsung Economic Research Institute. 2001. Three years after the IMF Bailout: A review of the korean economy's transformation since 1998. April, 39–40.

Shliefer, A., and R.W. Vishny. 1989. Management Entrenchment. *Journal of Financial Economies* 1: 123–139.

Walter, Andrew. 2008. *Governing Finance: East Asia's Adoption of International Standards*. Ithaca/London: Cornell University Press.

Williamson, Oliver E. 1994. The Institutions and Governance of Economic Development and Reform. *The World Bank Research Observer* 8: 171–197.

Yonhap News. September 12, 2015.

Chapter 4
Between Legalization and Democracy: A Transitional Irony of Informal Network

4.1 Introduction: What Has Caused the Informal Network to Proliferate?

In October 2007, a whistleblower from Samsung shocked South Korea. He claimed that Samsung disbursed so-called "*teokgap* (rice-cake expenses)" from illegal slush funds and bought off people with influence over policy making and enforcement, such as prosecutors, economic bureaucrats, academics, journalists, and politicians. They were, according to him, the network and the lobbying channel that protected Samsung. Large parts of the claim later turned out to be true. Although Korean society is known to be a network society of school ties, regional ties, family ties and kinship, this incident revealed a network that is unable to be explained using the social and cultural terms that previously explained Korea's network society. This incident, moreover, reignited both theoretical and practical debates on informal networks and the government-business relationship of Korea as it surfaced the *fait accompli* rumors regarding these practices of large corporations.

Has the developmental state of Korea, where, according to the relative autonomy or insulation thesis, the state is insulated and autonomous from the interests of the market or society, collapsed for certain? If it is, how is it done? Who is it done by? What strategy does business use? Who will win, the corporations or the government? These are some of the theoretical issues that were debated after the Asian Financial Crisis in 1997. But the incident in October 2007 cast philosophical and theoretical doubts on the expectations of increased transparency and responsibility in Korean society that seem to have resulted from the 1997 Asian Crisis and subsequent series of economic reforms. Why do informal networks grow more rapidly and extensively despite the successful progress of the democratization and globalization? Korea's democratization and globalization, which progressed through the democratic transition in 1987 and the economic crisis in 1997, have spread the discourse and idea of transparency and accountability. A series of political economic

S. Lee and S. Rhyu, *The Political Economy of Change and Continuity in Korea*,
The Political Economy of the Asia Pacific, https://doi.org/10.1007/978-3-319-71453-0_4

reforms, institutional changes, and legislation did, in fact, strengthen formality and the rule of law in Korea. But the incident in October 2007 raised fundamental questions regarding transparency, responsibility, and formality, as well as the need to reassess the role and limits of democracy and globalization, which had spread these discourses. It even suggests the possibility that informal networks may not be, in fact, abnormal, or that it may be too naïve and ideological to see informal networks as being paradoxical.

This study analyzes parachute appointment (*Nakhasan Insa*, the practice of the political appointment of politicians or retired high-ranking officials into public enterprises or private corporations in Korea), the typical informal network of Korea that is considered to be the hidden fabric of Korea's political economy as well as the main structural obstacle to enhancing transparency and responsibility. Why is parachute appointment, an informal network, increasing despite the decrease of the government's informal discretion and the increase of formality through economic reforms and legalization due to democratization and globalization?

Inquiry into specific facts is required in order to answer questions like this. Analysis of questions such as 'how are informal networks in Korea generated and sustained?' or 'what kind of political competition and economic interests are in play in the expansive reproduction of informal networks?' will be conducted. This study focuses on the paradox of Korea, where legalization works as the institutional environment that causes informal networks to proliferate through the concept of the legalization trap. The reality of parachute appointment will be theoretically analyzed through the case of Kim & Chang, the largest law firm in Korea. The operational mechanism of informal networks shown through the law firm, which is regarded as a symbol of the rule of law, legalization, and formality, will show an interesting cross section of where Korea's democracy and globalization stand now.

The rest of the study will be as follows. The second section will briefly give an overview of the theoretical debates on legalization and informal networks. It will assess the theoretical issues of the cause and effect of legalization and the relationship between globalization and democratization. Theoretical clues as to how legalization works as an environment that causes informal networks to proliferate will be sought. Korea's parachute appointment will be briefly compared with Japan's *Amakudari* (descent from heaven) and the revolving door of the U.S. The third section will provide an empirical analysis of how the parachute appointment, the typical informal network of Korea, has evolved until now. How the parachute appointment has been changed and reinforced, and what made this happen will be presented using detailed facts. The reorganization of parachute appointment through a number of market opportunities will be analyzed. The strategy of corporations to pull parachute appointments and the regulatory policy of the government will also be addressed. The fourth section will assess the reality of parachute appointment and the informal networks that are structured centering on the law firm of Kim & Chang. The legalization trap, where informal networks are strengthened while legalization is preceded, will be verified. The features and theoretical implications of Korea's informal networks will be presented in the concluding chapter.

4.2 Theoretical Overview: Globalization, Democratization and Legalization

Law and politics are indissolubly intertwined, and legalization is deeply embedded in politics. Douglass North, a neo-institutionalist, argued that "institutions explain everything until they explain nothing" (North 1990). Law, the core of formal institutions, evolves over time and issues. Numerous variables define how the close connection between law and politics operates. Law and institutions shape politics in a normal period, but during a critical juncture or an abnormal period, politics shape law and institutions. Law and institutions can constrain the strategic choices and interests of political players, while the political players change and re-design the law and institutions for their own interests and political ends. Thus, divergent paths of legalization have occurred in each country, and the form and substance taken in each case differs as well. What causes different types of legalization, and how do the political economic outcomes differ as a result?

In this era of globalization and democratic consolidation, we can witness a move towards law in many areas. Many international and domestic institutions have been legalized. The definition of international legalization contains three criteria: the degree to which rules are obligatory, the precision of those rules, and the delegation of some functions of interpretation, monitoring, and implementation to a third party (Goldstein et al. 2001, 3). In the same context, fully legalized domestic institutions bind all players to adhere to their rules through proscribed law. Legalized institutions also demonstrate a high degree of precision and formalization, meaning that their rules unambiguously and formally define the conduct they require, authorize, or proscribe. Greater legalization implies that behavior and process previously outside the scope of discretion and rule of politics is now within the scope of non-discretion and rule of law. The move to law includes the formalization of an informal practice or informal network in international and domestic politics (Abbott and Keohane et al. 2001, 17–35).

More discussions on legalization have occurred at the level of international politics. Legalization is spreading in various domains of international politics such as the WTO rules, Arms Control Agreement, and the recently created institution of FTAs. This expansion is, however, uneven throughout countries and numerous variations can be seen in the process. Why are the results of legalization uneven throughout countries? What creates divergence in the process of legalization? Who attempts to alter standing legalized institutions and why? These are the main issues. The realists, who emphasize power and state interests, see legalization as a minor factor, but the constructivists do not deny that legalized institutions might strengthen international identity or normative consensus. Institutionalists, although they regard law as a formal institution, have not directly addressed legalization, argue that legalization can improve institutional rationality and institutional endurance (Goldstein et al. 2001, 4–9).

Debates over the relationship among legalization, globalization, and democracy remain ongoing and lively among scholars who subscribe to each of these

Obligation	Expressly non-legal norm (informal practices and networks)	→	Binding rule (formal institutions and due process)
Precision	Vague principle with many exceptions	→	Precise, highly elaborated rule
Implementation	Discretionary rule of politics and rule of man	→	Nondiscretionary rule of law

Fig. 4.1 The dimensions of domestic legalization

perspectives. There can be debates over whether globalization caused legalization or legalization caused globalization. International legalization can constrain each country's domestic politics, and emphasize compliance, thereby expediting globalization, while it may also emphasize the limits of compliance and national sovereignty or domestic politics, thereby hampering globalization and democracy (Bieling 2008). In the same context, whether international legalization helps or hurts democracy in a specific country can be a theoretical issue (Gilbert 1999). Globalization and democracy are not necessarily complementary in their ideological foundations or strategic interests. How international legalization affects domestic reform, and how states mediate or comply with external pressure, is one of the traditional issues in political economy (Keohane et al. 1997; Cortell and Peterson 2002).

It is generally understood that legalization in domestic politics will help in consolidating democracy, as it will decrease the amount of discretion exercised by bureaucrats in the implementation and creation of policy and increase the rule of law. If reform means decreasing uncertainty and increasing predictability in politics and the market, legalization can be the formality and the substance of the reform. The rule of politics can be substituted with the rule of law as non-legal norms are transformed into binding rules, vague principles are stipulated as precise rules, and political deals are superseded by the legal process. Legalization can enhance transparency and accountability and take a positive role in promoting not only globalization but also democracy. A series of economic reforms Korea undertook since the 1997 Asian Crisis took the form of legalization, and are seen as having played a positive role in promoting Korea's democracy and globalization. This can be said to be the legalization process that builds a new model, where formal institution replaced Korea's previous economic model that was criticized for its informal practices and crony capitalism (Fig. 4.1).

Detailed political economic analysis on domestic legalization, however, is not easy to find, despite the numerous studies, from the viewpoint of new institutionalism, that have been written on the reforms in Korea. There is a wide consensus on the premise that legalization and globalization can promote democracy (Ginsburg 2004; Ginsburg 2012). Not much discussion has been had, however, on how legalization can contribute to globalization and democracy, what determines the paths of legalization, or the political competition and economic interests that occur in the process of legalization. For example, the paradox as to how informal networks are strengthening despite the spread of legalization remains unanswered.

Who leads the institutional transformation process and legalization, what domestic politics and reform path has the institutional change taken, what is the outcome, and what affects will it have on democracy? Charles Lindblom argues that democratic systems are dependent on the market and private enterprise (Lindblom 1977, 162). He then builds on this foundation to demonstrate the ways in which corporate power maintains control or at least has a significant amount of power in democratic systems. Lindblom argues that big business and corporations do not "fit" with the idea of democracy. According to him, democracy entails seeking private property rights and the freedom of enterprise, and it is not possible for politics, which pursues democratic values through regular elections, to consistently control the market. In the same context, it is eventually the power of market taking on the formality of the democratic system which leads institutional change and the legalization process. While democratic formality is maintained in its form, the path and the outcome of institutional change and legalization are, in the end, led by the market and corporations to serve their interests.

C. Wright Mills, meanwhile, takes a revisionist view and defines U.S. society as a society of the power elite, rather than a pluralistic society, as is traditionally argued. Mills examines the old moneyed classes in the United States, how the powerful and wealthy set up networks of influence through elite schools, and how the power elites recruited new members through such institutions as corporations and government service. In his book, "The Power Elite," Mills delivers a provocative examination of the nature of power, privilege, and status in the United States, explores how each of these three critical elements of power and property in this country are irrevocably connected to each other, and how they affect and determine the life chances and material hopes of ordinary human beings (Mills and Wolfe 2000). According to Mills, American society is no longer a democratic one where the middle class rules and pluralistic interests are achieved. It is, rather, a society where democratic values are damaged that is ruled by networks of power elites.

The study of Peter Gourevitch and James Shinn also provides valuable implications as they answer the question "why fight about corporate governance?" under the premise of "politics drives regulations, and regulations shape corporate governance patterns" (Gourevitch and Shinn 2005). Their book assesses the political process where interest groups collide over law and regulation. Various interest groups, owners, investors as outsiders and investors as insiders, workers as employees and workers as pension fund holders, managers of various kinds, so-called reputational intermediaries consisting of accountants, lawyers, bond-rating agencies, and institutional investors, fight through political institutions, the structure of which influence the outcomes. According to Gourevitch and Shinn, corporate governance structures are fundamentally the result of political decisions, and corporate governance systems reflect policy choices that are shaped by a mixture of laws, rules, regulations, and the degree of their enforcement (Gourevitch and Shinn 2005, 3). The internal political dynamics among institutions, preferences, parties and interest groups cause policy outcome variation within each country (Gourevitch and Shinn 2005, 12).

The writers argue that the degree of institutionalization of the institutions protecting the profits of minority shareholders is a barometer for the democratic features of corporate governance. They conclude that politics can play a role in weakening the power of corporations and strengthening democratic values by increasing regulations on corporate governance that protect minority shareholders. The economic reforms in Korea after the 1997 Asian Financial Crisis increased a variety of regulations to strengthen the responsibility of the major shareholder and to protect the profits of minority shareholders. This can be said to be the role of politics in strengthening democratic values and rules in the market.

Legalization is a process by which the scopes and power of formal institutions and formal and transparent networks are expanded by making the rules of politics and resource allocation adhere to formal law. The path and outcome of legalization in a given country, however, can be more imperceivably decided by informal politics and informal networks which are deeply embedded in society. The power and scope of informal politics and networks are not necessarily reduced or weakened as the power and scope of formal institutions and networks expand due to legalization. Rather, informal networks tend to expand and be reorganized exquisitely in order for stakeholders to continue to pursue political competition and economic benefits under the changed constraints of legalization. It is the primary aim of this study, therefore, to analyze how formal legalization and informal networks interact, and how the path and outcome of legalization are formed by informal networks (Fig. 4.2).

Parachute appointment symbolizes the informal network in Korea. Parachute appointment is a type of informal network where politicians or retired high-ranked bureaucrats are employed in high-paying positions in public or private enterprises that are part of the industry the appointee was previously in charge of regulating, and perform as a window through which information or political pressure are channeled (Lee and Rhyu 2008). The president or the leadership of the ruling party appoints the politicians on their side who yielded or lost in elections to these executive positions, such as the position of head or auditor of a public enterprise, as a form of economic compensation. These appointments also create a political support basis for the administration. Retired high-ranked bureaucrats circumvent through career laundering the legal restriction which forbids politicians or bureaucrats from being re-employed by the industry they were previously in charge of for a period of 2 years following their exit from the government. Through parachute appointment, they are re-employed by the industry they previously oversaw, which incapacitates the monitoring and regulating functions of the government in the industry, and affects the policy decision making process of the government regarding private enterprises. This kind of informal network decreases trust in and

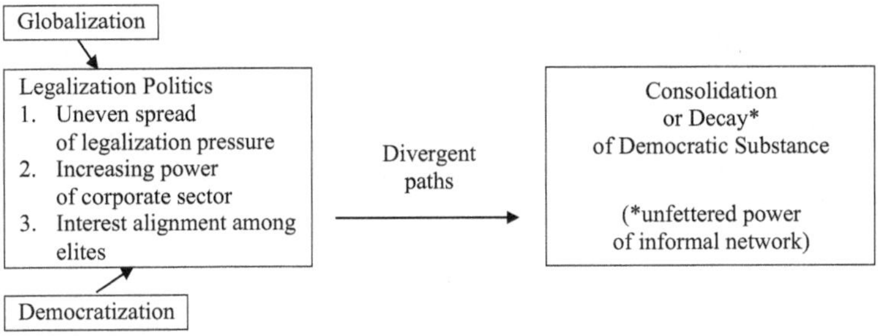

Fig. 4.2 Conceptual framework: Legalization politics and democracy

transparency of government policy and causes distortion in political representation and the distribution of economic resources, thus weakening the function of Korea's overall democracy.

The theoretical discourse on legalization and informal networks is related to the debate over the dissolution of the East Asian developmental state. The dominant view is that the traditional developmental state in East Asia is now completely dissolved due to the pressure of globalization and the proliferation of legalization, and weakening informal networks and proliferating legalization is the key to economic reform and the shortcut to a new economic model. It is intellectually compelling that if the East Asian countries are pressured to completely comply with global standards, the developmental state will be dissolved and both globalization and democracy will be intensified. But, as seen in the mock-compliance discourse, informal networks die hard. The form has changed and dissolved, but the substance remains without a big change. It is witnessed that as formal law emerges in China and Japan, there is a growing complementarity between the formal institutions of the legal system and the informal rules and norms of *guanxi* and *amakudari* relations (Gold et al. 2008, 19; Colignon and Usui 2003; Grimes 2001; Rhyu 2007). It is the legalization trap, or an ironic phenomenon that can be found in any given society. The animated debates on the post-developmental state cannot progress further without assessing the interaction of legalization and informal networks.

4.3 The Historical Evolution of Informal Networks

Parachute appointment, Korea's primary informal network, began with the birth of the developmental state. The Park Chung-hee government, born as the result of the 1961 *coup d'état*, placed former military politicians and high-ranking bureaucrats who had special ties with the President and the ruling party in public enterprises, government banks, and private enterprises in order to efficiently execute the industrial policies and support the administration beginning in the 1960s. This trend, where the largest portion of the parachute appointment was comprised of former military personnel, lasted until the Chun Doo-hwan administration during the mid-1980s (Kim 2003; Kim and Lee 2001). Parachute appointment and informal networks still persist in spite of the economic reforms following the 1997 Asian Crisis.

We can, however, see that the composition of parachute appointment and its reproduction mechanism have gone through distinctive changes. The structural change of the political economy due to the democratic transition in 1987 and the Asian Crisis in 1997 has brought about changes to the personnel composition of parachute appointments. Recent cases show that the pull factor of the corporations is more strongly affecting the process than the push factor of the government. Corporations are adopting the strategy of recruiting more parachute appointment personnel from departments related to legal issues as they accommodate themselves to the increasing legalization that is a result of the 1997 Asian financial crisis. It is observed that a new form of informal network is now being built among the bureaucrats, law firms, and private enterprises as the law firms increasingly employ retired high-ranked bureaucrats as their lobbying channel and legalization proliferates. This is a significant change in comparison to the traditional form of informal networks, where politicians employed by public enterprises made up the majority of parachute appointments.

The absolute number of parachute appointments in public enterprises has declined significantly in the 2000s. However, this does not necessarily imply that the importance of parachute appointment has decreased. This decrease basically resulted from the reduction of the total number of director positions in the wake of public-sector reform following the 1997 Asian Crisis. Through the "Government-Affiliated Institutions Management Law" promulgated in February of 1999, two director positions in each public enterprise were abolished. However, regardless of political regimes, the overall percentage of parachute appointments for the president, the chief directors, and the auditors has been relatively stable for the entire period, hovering at around 80% (Lee 2014). Despite mounting public criticism of parachute appointment and a heightened demand for public sector reform, the practice of parachute appointment in Korea did not substantially weaken in the earlier days of the Roh Moo-hyun government.

Parachute appointments to public enterprises tended to be strengthened during the Lee Myung-bak administration and the Park Geun-hye administration that succeeded it has followed this trend. Both presidents pledged to eradicate parachute appointment when they were running for office, but neither kept their promises. At the beginning of the Lee Myung-bak administration's tenure, National Assemblyman Ahn Kyeong-ryul, the secretary general of the ruling party at the time, made a statement regarding parachute appointments, saying "to properly honor the people who endeavored to create the administration is an inevitable side of the party democracy" (*Joongang Sunday*, July 20, 2008). Lee Myung-bak administration appointed 306 politicians and supporters of Lee Myung-bak to 186 out of the 284 public institutions within 3 years of its inauguration (Min 2014). It was a great increase compared to the appointment of 185 politicians and supporters to 125 institutions over the 5-year tenure of during Roh Moo-hyun administration (www.alio.go.kr, searched date: 05 April 2014).

Table 4.1 Increasing parachute appointments in the legalization area

	1982	1996	1997	1998	1999	2000	2001	2002	2003
1	MOCT (36)	MOF (64)	MOF (57)	MOF (52)	NTS (48)	NTS (59)	NTS (60)	NTS (56)	NTS (66)
2	MOF (34)	MND (41)	MND (36)	MOJ (28)	MOJ (41)	MOF (43)	MOF (43)	MOF (43)	MOF (53)
3	MOIT (16)	MOCT (23)	PO (14)	MNC (27)	MOF (40)	MOJ (41)	MOJ (38)	MOJ (40)	FSC (45)
4	MOHA (15)	MOFAT (16)	MOCT (11)	TA (24)	FSC (25)	FSC (34)	FSC (33)	FSC (35)	MOJ (44)
5	MOA (9)	PO (14)	MOIT (11)	PO (18)	MND (19)	MND (34)	MND (25)	MND (28)	MND (32)
Top 3	55.8	55.4	58.8	48.9	50.0	45.1	45.2	43.4	45.2
Top 5	71.4	68.4	70.9	68.0	67.1	64.6	63.8	63.1	66.1

Source: Kim and Lee 2001; Korea Listed Companies Association, *Who's Who of Listed Companies in Korea (1996–2003)*

The Park Geun-hye administration appointed 114 politicians and supporters to 84 institutions within just 1 year of its inauguration in 2013. 55 were affiliated with the ruling Saenuri Party, 40 were from the presidential campaign camp, and 46 of them were presidential campaign activists (Min 2014). Among the presidents of the public institutions that Park Geun-hye administration appointed during the last year, only 15% were promoted from within and the other 85% were parachute appointments (*The Kyunghyang Shinmun*, February 24, 2014). As President Park announced that she will replace the presidents of the institutions with the "people who share the philosophy of the administration," the number of parachute appointments made by this administration is likely to increase compared to its predecessors, and it can be confirmed that the proportion of politicians, in at least those serving in public institutions via parachute appointment, is rising.

The number of parachute appointments by each major ministry shows the changes in the strategy of corporations and personnel composition of parachute appointments as a reaction to legalization. The surge in personnel of Ministry of Justice and National Tax Service after 1999 can be understood in this context, as it occurred when the results of the reforms increasing legalization after 1997 began to bear fruit. The numbers are, of course, affected by the separation of the Financial Supervisory Commission from the Ministry of Finance, but they also show the shift in corporate strategies as companies reacted to a new political economic environment and institutional restraints put in place through legalization (Table 4.1).

The institutionalization of the Korean economy was promoted by a series of neoliberal economic reforms and institutional changes which occurred after the Asian financial crisis in 1997. The rule of politics and discretionary administrative regulation, which defined the government-business relationship, was replaced with more precisely defined formal institutions and non-discretionary rule of law. The method used by the state to control corporations also shifted from political threats and disadvantages that mobilized physical power to economic disadvantages, such as tax investigations or capital punishment (Lee and Rhyu 2008; Lee and Rhyu 2014).

Large businesses employed more influential people with expertise, experience, and networks in law and taxation, as the legalization put into place via reforms meant that disputes and discord between the government and corporations was no longer settled through administrative compromises or political coordination, but via lawsuits and legal judgments. Corporations, on the one hand, utilized their informal networks in order to minimize institutional constraints and market uncertainty that legalization brought them and, on the other, strengthened informal lobbying to both the legislature and the executive branches of the government to directly influence the legalization process in order to design formal institutions that will ensure maximization of their profits. The legalization trap through dynamic politics, where domestic legalization strengthened informal networks, occurred.

4.4 The Politics of Legalization and Informal Networks: The Case of Kim & Chang

The case of Kim & Chang, the largest law firm in Korea, symbolically shows the reorganization process of informal networks and the paradox of the legalization trap that occurs in the process. Kim & Chang started out in 1972 and rapidly grew as it represented large domestic corporations as well as global corporations such as the Chase Manhattan Bank and Citibank in the 1980s. After the crisis in 1997, Kim & Chang grew in both size and expertise in dealing with the economic reforms, corporate restructuring, and the selling of corporations to overseas buyers. By 2012, the firm consisted of more than 580 lawyers, including members of overseas bars, and the number exceeds 800 if patent attorneys and tax accountants are included. It has the largest sales amount among Korean law firms. It is the only Korean law firm to be listed in the Who's Who Legal 100 of 2013 and the only Korean law firm to be listed as Band 1 in all 14 subsections of the Legal 500 Asia Pacific 2014.

Kim & Chang is taking a new path in the informal networks of Korea. It has enormous influence over the legalization and the institutional reform process as it employs retired high-ranking bureaucrats as expert members or advisors. It helps the lawyers or the retired high-ranking bureaucrats they employed advance to the key posts in the administration or the outside director of the large corporations (*Chaebols*) (Table 4.2).

In 2010, the top 6 law firms who had the most sales in M&As in Korea were Kim & Chang, Bae, Kim & Lee, Shin & Kim, Lee & Ko, Yulchon, and Yoon & Yang. In that year 19 (19.79%) personnel who were not lawyers from the Fair Trade Commission were employed to those law firms. The Financial Supervisory Service (including the Financial Services Commission) had the second largest number of personnel (18) hired and the National Tax Service (including the Korea Customs Service) followed with 16. The experts from these three agencies comprised 55.2% of the parachute appointments in 2010, with 53 people.

Table 4.2 Parachute appointment in the top 6 Korean Law Firms by Institutional and Job Origin (2010)

Affiliated institution before employment	Number of people	Proportion (%)
Fair Trade Commission (FTC)	19	19.79
Financial Supervisory Service (FSS)/Financial Services Commission (FSC)	18	18.75
National Tax Services (NTS)/Korea Customs Service (KCS)	16	16.67
State-owned Financial Institutions	8	8.33
Other government ministries/Public officials in government agencies	25	26.04
Businessman	3	3.13
Politicians	3	3.13
Others	5	4.17
Total	96	100

Source: Citizen's Coalition for Economic Justice, Press Release (May 18, 2011)

The large law firms are shown to employ more parachute appointees from the three government agencies against whom the corporations file lawsuits, as the large law firms tend to represent the large corporations in those suits. This confirms that legalization since the economic crisis has provided the opportunity to expansively reproduce informal networks. The increase of parachute appointees from the Fair Trade Commission seems to be the result of the strengthening of informal networks as the implementation of antitrust laws became more stringent with legalization and its heightened emphasis on fair competition. The sharp increase in the number of parachute appointees from the National Tax Service and the Korea Customs Service can be understood in the same context. This tendency in the top 6 law firms can more apparently be witnessed in the parachute appointment of expert members or advisors in Kim & Chang in 2007 (Table 4.3).

A new form of informal network can be found, meanwhile, centered on the law firms, as lawyers or retired high-ranking bureaucrats employed by Kim & Chang become appointed as outside directors of large corporations such as Samsung and Hyundai. It is different from the traditional informal network, as traditional networks existed between the government and corporations. This new form of informal network is created by the voluntary pull of the corporations, not the push from the government, to minimize the uncertainty of the market. It is, especially, pointed out that the large corporations appoint outside directors from the large law firms as a windbreaker against their pending cases over allegations such as management rights succession-related illegality, accounting fraud, slush funds, or lawsuits against the National Tax Service or the Fair Trade Commission (Kim 2008). The corporations lobby the members of the National Assembly or their aides, or hire the former staffers to the members of the National Assembly to lobby for them in order to include their interests into the legislation (*CBS Nocut News*, April 7, 2014). This is also a new phenomenon which followed the proliferation of the legalization (Table 4.4).

Kim & Chang had both direct and indirect influence over the policy decision making, as its lawyers and the retired high-ranked bureaucrats that it employed were

Table 4.3 Retired officials who moved to the Law Firm, Kim & Chang

Department	Numbers	Major positions
Ministry of Strategy and Finance (MSF)	9	Minister(1), Director of Finance(1)
National Tax Service (NTS)	22	Commissioner(1), Regional Commissioner(4)
Korea Customs Service (KCS)	5	Commissioner(1)
Financial Supervisory Service (FSS)	6	Director of Credit Supervision(1)
Fair Trade Commission (FTC)	7	Vice Chairman(1)
Ministry of Knowledge Economy (MKE)	6	Consul General in Shanghai(1)
Ministry of Employment and Labor (MOEL)	3	Director of Seoul Regional Office(1)
Office of the President	3	Senior Secretary of the President for Civil Affairs(1)
Others	Ministry of Foreign Affairs(1), Government Policy Coordination(1), Ministry of Culture, Sports and Tourism(2), Ministry of Health and Welfare(2), Audit(2)	

Source: Lim and Chang (2008)

appointed, or re-appointed, to key positions in the administration as the regime changed. For example, Prime Minister Han Duk-soo, who served under Roh Moo-hyun, and Prime Minister Han Seung-soo, who served under Lee Myung-bak, were all appointed from Kim & Chang. The rate of appointments from Kim & Chang to key government posts spiked during Lee Myung-bak administration as the administration put more emphasis on corporate-friendly policies and less on the ethics of the civil servant (Table 4.5).

The Secretary to the President for Public Office Discipline, who oversees the duties of and tracks corruption among public officials, the President of the Constitutional Court, one of the highest constitutional institutions whose jurisdiction is directly related to legalization, were appointed from Kim & Chang. There also was an attempt to appoint a lawyer from Kim & Chang who represented large corporations to the position of Chairman of the Fair Trade Commission, a post that observes large corporations and prevents monopolies from forming. Although this attempt failed due to harsh criticism from both the ruling and opposition parties, it was an incident that symbolized the extent to which Kim & Chang's informal network had become deeply and structurally rooted into Korean society. Kim & Chang introduces itself as "providing legal service with the experience and knowledge on

Table 4.4 Outside directors of major businesses affiliated to Kim & Chang (September, 2007)

Group	Company	Outside director	Position at Kim & Chang
Samsung	Samsung Engineering	Kim Cheolmin	Certified Tax Accountant (Former Superintendent of Namdaemun District Tax Office)
	Samsung Securities	Lee Joo-seuk	Senior Advisor (Former Commissioner of Seoul Regional Tax Office)
	Samsung Electronics	Hwang Jae Sung	Senior Advisor (Former Commissioner of Seoul Regional Tax Office)
		Yoon Dong-min	Attorney (Former Project Manager of the Office of Planning and Coordination of the Ministry of Justice)
Hyundai Motor	Hyundai Autonet	Han Sang Ho	Attorney (Former Chief Prosecuting Attorney of the Seoul Central District Court)
	Hyundai Mobis	Choi ByungChul	Senior Advisor (Former Commissioner for Corporate Taxation of the National Tax Service)
	Hyundai Steel	Choi Kyung-Won	Attorney (Former Minister of Justice)
		Chon Hyung Soo	Senior Advisor (Former Commissioner of Seoul Regional Tax Office)
	Hyundai Glovis	Lee Jeong-soo	Attorney (Former Assistant Prosecutor General of the Supreme Prosecutor's Office)

Source: Lim and Chang (2008)

Table 4.5 Major personnel who moved to Lee Myung-bak government as high ranking officials from the Law Firm of Kim & Chang

Personnel affiliated with Kim & Chang	Appointed position
Han Seung-soo, Senior Advisor	Prime Minister
Yoon Jeung-hyun, Senior Advisor	Minister of Strategy and Finance
Lee Jae-hoon, Senior Advisor	Nominee for Minister of Knowledge Economy
Park Han-Chul, Attorney	Justice of the Constitutional Court of Korea
Kim Hoe-sun, Attorney	Second Deputy Chief of the National Intelligence Service
Seo Dong-won, Senior Advisor	Chairman of the Fair Trade Commission
Park In-jae, Attorney	Vice Chairman of the Anti-Corruption and Civil Rights Commission
Kwon Do-yeop, Senior Advisor	Minister of Land, Infrastructure and Transport
Cho Yoon-Sun, Attorney	Spokesperson of Grand National Party (currently the Saenuri Party)
Kim Eunhae's husband, Attorney	Vice Spokesperson of the Blue House (*Cheongwadae*)
Han Duk-soo, Senior Advisor	Ambassador to the United States
Jang Yongseok, Attorney	Secretary to the President for Civil Affairs of the Blue House
Lee Jae-Ho, Attorney	Secretary for Legal Affairs to the Office to the President for Civil Affairs
Chung Jin-Young, Attorney	Senior Secretary to the President for Civil Affairs

Source: http://impeter.tistory.com/ (searched date: 05 April 2014)

the law itself and its practices, obtained through participating in the legislative process from drafting laws and the amendment process" (Lim and Chang 2008). This is only possible through strong informal networks, not through formal institutions.

The case of Seo Dong-won, the Vice Chairman of the Fair Trade Commission during the Lee Myung-bak administration, elaborates the operation mechanism of Kim & Chang's informal network. Seo joined Kim & Chang 4 months after he retired as Standing Commissioner of the Fair Trade Commission in May 2006. He led the sanctions against Microsoft as the chief on the 'Microsoft Monopoly Case.' After retiring from the Fair Trade Commission, he, as an advisor to Kim & Chang, advised on the case wherein Microsoft demanded a withdrawal of the fine and a correction order (http://impeter.tistory.com/, searched date: 22 August 2011). Kim & Chang is called a law firm, but it is registered as an association among individual lawyers rather than as a unitary law firm. This places Kim & Chang under fewer constraints compared to the other law firms that are registered as a law firm. This also allows the lawyers of Kim & Chang to represent both the defendants and the plaintiffs in a single case. For example, Kim & Chang represented both Lone Star Funds, the seller, and Kookmin Bank, the buyer, in the resale case of the Korean Exchange Bank in 2003 and concluded the M&A. Kim & Chang is free from legal restraints and is the only example of a law firm that is able to legally perform as the legal representative for both sides. This gives Kim & Chang a wide amount of room to maneuver within their informal network.

There are paradoxical assertions that it was under relatively progressive administrations, the Kim Dae-jung administration and the Roh Moo-hyun administration that Kim & Chang rapidly grew and expanded (Lim and Chang 2008). Legalization proliferated as the result of a series of economic reforms due to the pressures of neo-liberalism and globalization after the economic crisis in 1997. The interest alignments among the elites to adapt to the transforming situation seem to have strengthened the informal network. The legalization pressure in Korea after the Asian financial crisis was an uneven spread favoring the promotion of globalization through large corporations rather than the consolidation of democracy founded in civil society. The initial goal of the economic reform was to enhance the responsibility and transparency of large corporations. But this goal was only reflected in formal institutions and failed to reform customary, informal practices. Moreover, the interest alignment among the elites such as large domestic corporations, foreign capital, and bureaucrats allowed the elites to legally seek rent within the form of legalization. This resulted in democratic decay.

As the harms resulting from informal networks and parachute appointments became more frequently highlighted as a problematic issue, both the Public Service Ethics Act and the Attorney-at-law Act were strengthened to regulate parachute appointment (Kim 2014). It is, nonetheless, impossible to completely control an informal network that has its structural roots in the policy decision making process. This tendency continued with the Park Geun-hye administration. The U.S. has witnessed the repeating scenario where the revolving door expands due to new business booms or the appearance of new opportunities to seek rent but then diminishes as society criticizes its expansion and strengthens the legal institutions that oversee the revolving door (Meghani and Kuzma 2011). The 1948 Criminal Code Amendment strengthening the 2 years of regulation period, wherein a bureaucrat should wait before being eligible for appointment to a revolving door position, was intended to regulate the booming revolving door in government supply that expanded during the Second World War, and the Ethics in Government Act of 1978 was passed due to a series of failures in regulation following the end of 1960s and the Watergate Scandal (Mundheim 1981, 711–713; Burger 2006). But it is hard to eliminate informal networks unless legalization politics change as a whole. There is always the possibility that legalization can harm the substance of democracy.

4.5 Conclusion

The politics of legalization determines the relationship and interactions between legalization and democracy. The possibility of informal networks strengthening rapidly and democratic substance decaying increases when the expansion of legalization unevenly proceeds in favor of globalization, which can run counter to democracy in its values. It is also possible during the process of democratic consolidation when the power of the corporations is stronger than that of the state, and the balance of elites among the corporations and government breaks and an exclusive interest alignment is formed amongst them. The case of parachute appointment and the strengthening of the informal networks of Kim & Chang in Korea present an example of how legalization can hamper democracy. The future of democracy in Korea will be decided by who, when, how, and what breaks the path-dependence of informal networks and legalization trap.

References

Abbott, Kenneth W., Robert O. Keohane, Andrew Moravcsik, Anne-Marie Slaughter, and Duncan Snidal. 2001. The concept of legalization. In *Legalization and world politics*, ed. Judith Goldstein, Miles Kahler, Robert O. Keohane, and Anne-Marie Slaughter. Cambridge: MIT.

ALI Public Information in One at <www.alio.go.kr.> (searched date: 05 April 2014).

Bieling, Hans-Jürgen. 2008. The Other Side of the Coin: Conceptualization the Relationship between Business and the State in the Age of Globalization. *Business and Politics* 9 (3): 1–22.

Burger, Timothy J. 2006. The Lobbying Game: Why the Revolving Door Won't Close. *TIME*. February 16.

CBS Nocut News. April 7, 2014.

Citizen's Coalition for Economic Justice, Press Release (May 18, 2011).

Colignon, Richard A., and Chikako Usui. 2003. *Amakudari: The Hidden Fabric of Japan's Economy*. New York: Cornell University Press.

Cortell, Andrew P., and Susan Peterson, eds. 2002. *Altered States: International Relations, Domestic Politics, and Institutional Change*. Lanham: Lexington.

Gilbert, Alan. 1999. *Must Global Politics Constrain Democracy?: Great-Power Realism, Democratic Peace, and Democratic Internationalism*. Princeton: Princeton University Press.

Ginsburg, Tom. 2004. *Legal Reform in Korea*. New York: Routledge.

———, ed. 2012. *Legal Reform in Korea*. London: Routledge Curzon.

Gold, Thomas, Doug Guthrie, and David Wank. 2008. An Introduction to the Study of Guanxi. In *Social Connections in China: Institutions, Culture, and the Changing Nature of Guanxi*, ed. Thomas Gold, Doug Guthrie, and David Wank, 3–20. New York: Cambridge University Press.

Goldstein, Judith, Miles Kahler, Robert O. Keohane, and Anne-Marie Slaughter, eds. 2001. *Legalization and World Politics*. Cambridge: MIT.

Gourevitch, Peter Alexis, and James Shinn. 2005. *Political Power and Corporate Control: The New Global Politics of Corporate Governance*. Princeton: Princeton University Press.

Grimes, William W. 2001. *Unmaking the Japanese Miracle: Macroeconomic Politics, 1985–2000*. New York: Cornell University Press.

Joongang Sunday. July 20, 2008.

Keohane, Robert O., Andrew Moravcsik, and Anne-Marie Slaughter. 1997. *Toward a theory of legalization*. Paper presented at the Conference on International Law and Domestic Politics in California, U.S.A., June.

Kim, Nam-sun. 2008 High ranking officials going directly to law firms and large conglomerates. *Chosun Monthly*. September. 80–93.

Kim, Pan Suk. 2003. Jeongbu Sanhakikwanei Siltaewa Kwanri Hyoyulwha Bangan Yeongu. [Study on Sub-Government Institutions' Organizational Efficiency]. *Study on Korean Society and Administration* 13 (4): 43–70. (in Korean).

Kim, Yong Min, and Su Il Lee. 2001. Jeongkun Kyocheae Darun Sangjangsa Imwonui Jiwui Byundong. [Executive Level Personnel's Position Change in Listing Companies According to Administration Change], *Korean Strategic Management Society*, November 23. (in Korean).

Kim, Youngho. "Strengthened Limitations on Reemployment of 'Retired Public Officials'." *NTN*, April 25, 2014. Web.

Korea Listed Companies Association. Who's Who of Listed Companies in Korea (1996–2003)

Lee, Seungjoo, and Sang-young Rhyu. 2008. The Political Dynamics of Informal Networks in South Korea: The Case of Parachute Appointment. *The Pacific Review* 21 (1): 45–66.

———. 2014. The Political Economy of Informal Networks in Japan and South Korea: Amakudari vs. Parachute Appointment. In *A Comparative Study of East Asian Capitalism. Berkeley: Institute of east Asian Studies*, ed. Hong Yung Lee, 261–282. Berkeley: University of California.

Lee, Won-joo. 2014. 4 Out of 10 Outside Directors of Top 10 Companies Originate From 'Power Institutions'. *DongA News* (March 10) Web.

Lim, Jong-in, and Hwa-sik Chang. 2008. *Beobryulsamuso Gim'anjang*. [The Law Firm Kim & Chang] Seoul: Humanities.

Lindblom, Charles. 1977. *Politics and Markets*. New York: Basic Books.

Meghani, Zahra, and Jennifer Kuzma. 2011. The "Revolving Door" between Regulatory Agencies and Industry: A Problem That Requires Reconceptualizing Objectivity. *Journal of Agricultural & Environmental Ethics* 24: 575–599.

Mills, C. Wright, and Alan Wolfe. 2000. *The Power Elite*. London: Oxford University Press.

Min, Byung Doo. 2014. *Who's Who of Park's Supports in Public Institutions*. Unpublished Report. (in Korean).

Mundheim, Robert H. 1981. Conflict of Interest and the Former Government Employee: Rethinking the Revolving Door. *Creighton Law Review* 14: 707–721.

North, Douglass C. 1990. *Institutions, Institutional Change and economic Performance*. New York: Cambridge University Press.

Rhyu, Sang-young. 2007. Determining the Existence of Amakudari in Publicly-traded Japanese Companies. *Applied Economics Letters,* 15(14) (October). 1097-11-3.

The Kyunghyang Shinmun. February 24, 2014.

Chapter 5
The Dual Dynamics of the IT Industry Transformation

5.1 Introduction

Since the late 1990s, the development of the information and telecommunication (IT) Korean industry has been often cited as a case showing the Korean economy's adaptive capacity under the rapidly shifting domestic and international environments. In particular, the autonomous development of the Time Division Exchange (TDX) and the commercialization of the Code Division Multiple Access (CDMA) are touted as an example of the successful execution of Korea's catch-up strategy in the IT industry. The IT industry also became a locomotive reviving the Korean economy in the aftermath of the financial crisis of 1997. In 1996, the industrial output of the IT industry was 5729 billion won, accounting for 11.9% of the Korean GDP. Within the entire IT industry, the ICT equipment production was dominant with a total output of 3.68 trillion won, while other telecommunication service, broadcasting service, and software took 1.17 trillion won, 299 billion won, and 259 billion won, respectively.

Despite the Asian financial crisis, the Korean IT industry continued to grow without serious interruption. In 1997, the IT industry's industrial output increased by 26% to reach 7.22 trillion won. In 1999, the IT industry's total output exceeded 11 trillion won, accounting for 19.7% of the Korean GDP. In the 2000s, outstanding growth of the IT industry continued. As indicated in Fig. 5.1, in 2014, the IT industry accounts for 30.3% of the Korean GDP with the total output of 44.9 trillion won (National Index homepage, http://www.index.go.kr/potal/stts/idxMain/selectPoSttsIdxSearch.do?idx_cd=2888). From 1997 to 2014, average annual growth rate of the IT industry was 16%. Given that Korea's average annual GDP growth rate was 4.6% during the same period, the growth of the IT industry was indeed remarkable. However, the unbalanced nature of the IT industry did not change. In 2014, IT equipment production was still dominant with the share of 62.8%. The share of telecommunications service, broadcasting service, and software were about 10%, 3%, and 8.3% (National Index homepage, http://www.index.go.kr/potal/stts/idxMain/selectPoSttsIdxSearch.do?idx_cd=2888).

S. Lee and S. Rhyu, *The Political Economy of Change and Continuity in Korea*,
The Political Economy of the Asia Pacific, https://doi.org/10.1007/978-3-319-71453-0_5

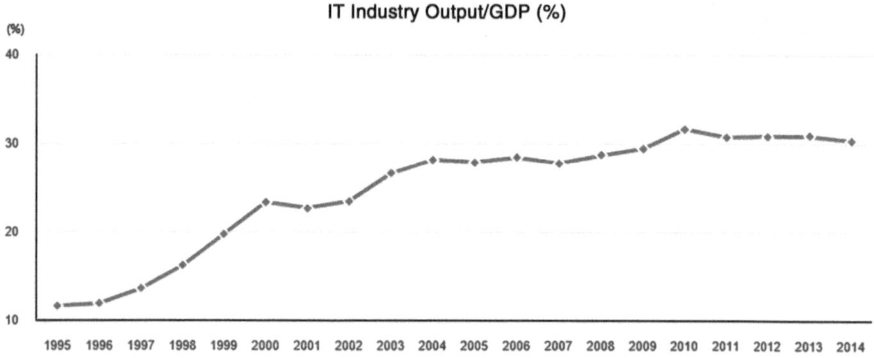

Fig. 5.1 IT Industry's GDP Share (1995–2014) (Source: https://www.index.go.kr/potal/stts/idxMain/selectPoSttsIdxMainPrint.do?idx_cd=2888&board_cd=INDX_001#link)

The stellar performance of the Korean IT industry was made possible because the Korean government could create a cozy and effective governance among manufacturing companies, service providers and government-affiliated research institutes. A stable policy network forged among them was an institutional arrangement underpinning the success of the Korean IT industry. With this institutional advantage, Korea could successfully emerge as a global player in the IT industry. Various international organizations such as the organization Economic Cooperation and Development (OECD) and the International Telecommunication Union (ITU) also praised outstanding performance of the Korean IT industry (Ministry of Information and Communication 2003: 21). For example, OECD ranked the Korean IT industry's competitiveness 6th among the 28 member countries, following the US, Finland, Sweden, the UK (*Etnews* September 3, 2003). In February 2017, the KT announced an ambitious plan to introduce world' first 5G commercial service (*Dong-A Daily* 2/28/2017).

5.2 The Korean Government Strategy

Since the 1990s, the Korean government played a central role in every stage of the IT industry development by successfully combining promotion and liberalization. In the face of new challenges such as the increasing pressure from the forces of globalization and market opening, and structural adjustment in the aftermath of the Asian financial crisis, the Korean government attempted to transform itself, departing away from the traditional model of the development state (Weiss 2000). Lacking resources available to the previous governments during the high growth period, the Korean developmental state had to find new institutional arrangements in structuring the relations between various players such as IT manufacturing companies, IT services providers, and research institutes.

In this chapter, I attempt to demonstrate the way in which the Korean government pushed for strategic liberalization since the early 1990s to nurture the industry as well as created an eco-system where various players and stakeholders formed and maintained a cozy relationship among themselves. First, as external – bilateral and multilateral – pressures to open up the Korean market in the IT industry increased since the late 1980s, the Korean government thought it was inevitable to liberalize the IT industry. The liberalization was not a matter of 'whether or not,' but a matter of 'how.' The gist of the Korean government's strategy was craft competitive market environments in preparation for market opening to foreign firms. For this goal, the Korean government had to fundamentally rearrange the relationship between local companies and global production networks (Evans 1995; Yeung 2014). In contrast to typical liberalization, however, the liberalization process was led by the government. In general, liberalization is expected to accompany the retreat of the state because it is unavoidable for the government to reduce intervention into the market. Rather, the Korean government led liberalization by taking an initiative in designing the overall strategies in every critical stage.

The first task the Korean government had to address was figure out interest configuration in the IT industry. To mobilize support for liberalization, it was needed to identify players who would benefit from liberalization (Rogowski 1990; Milner 1988). However, because it was not an easy task to make a distinction between beneficiaries and victims of liberalization, the Korean government was in trouble in garnering support from major players. Although they could benefit from liberalization in general, major IT manufacturers and services providers were cautious. Recognizing that they were not fully competitive vis-à-vis foreign companies, the manufacturers and services providers thought it was better to delay liberalization. Moreover, because *chaebols* that were the major players in the IT industry were highly diversified, they were ambivalent in speeding up liberalization, fearing that the liberalization drive may spill over other relatively non-competitive industrial sectors. *Chaebols* could be beneficiaries as well as victims of liberalization, given that they diversified into various industrial sectors. In that regard, interest configuration was complex and not friendly in pushing for early liberalization of the IT industry.

Nonetheless, the Korean government decided to proceed liberalization. Four factors helped the Korean government lead liberalization by fending off societal pressure opposing liberalization. First, the Asian financial crisis became a catalyst that precipitated structural changes in Korea. The crisis brought about profound impact not just on the economic system but on socio-political foundations of the developmental state model (MacIntyre, Pempel and Ravenhill 2008). The Asian financial crisis was a watershed in terms of political economy model of Korea. While the developmental state model was an institutional foundation that spearheaded Korea's rapid economic growth since the 1960s, it was essentially a catch-up model, revealing the limitations in adapting to new challenges arising from both internal and external changes such as globalization and democratization.

Second, while the Asian financial crisis was a direct cause of discarding the past developmental model, ideological shift both within the political leadership and the bureaucracy served as a guide for the direction of institutional transformation. The general consensus was formed within the political leadership and bureaucracy that it was about time to creatively reconstruct a new model of development to upgrade the Korean economy to the next level. Although the IMF program imposed on the Korean government in return for provision of rescue fund did eliminate the crucial elements of the existing developmental model, it did not specify the nature of the future model of development. Moreover, ideological shift away from the past developmentalism, combined with the political predilection to join the OECD, preceded reform drives arranged with the IMF (Thurbon 2001). It is indeed true that the Asian financial crisis put a great deal of pressure on the Kim Dae-jung government to make a fundamental change toward liberalization, departing from the past legacies of developmentalism. The liberalization process of the IT industry is a good case in point to demonstrate the way in which ideological shift played out, in the sense that the bureaucracy essentially took an initiative in liberalization of the IT sector rather than solely immersed in expanding its bureaucratic control.

Third, the interplay between external and internal pressure was at the core of institutional transformation. The Kim Dae-jung government faced a daunting challenge as forces of globalization and democratization unfolded simultaneously in Korea. On the one hand, the Kim government had to deal with external pressures to restructure the Korean economic system, moving to a system similar to the neoliberal model. On the other hand, the Kim government also faced serious internal, sometimes conflicting, pressures from private actors such as businesses and domestic activist groups to secure their respective interests in the newly established model. Rather than being subject to external pressure unconditionally, the Kim government substantially modified and shaped to create a new model of development. Under the circumstance, the Kim government strategically utilized external pressure to deal with domestic actors. Juxtaposed between external and internal forces, the Korean government was in a unique position to mediate them. As demonstrated in the case of *chaebol* reform, the Korean government could enhance its capability vis-à-vis domestic interest groups and successfully preempted their potential opposition. In so doing, the Korean government could dictate the course of the institutional transformation rather than being squeezed between both sides.

Fourth, when it comes to the IT sector, the Korean government in advance of mounting external pressures strategically made preemptive decisions to lead an institutional transformation that in turn contributed to designing the nature, scope and speed of liberalization. The fact that initial restructuring took place under the Kim Young-sam government suggests the Korean government's preemptive move. The Kim Young-sam government embarked on the government restructuring to streamline the policymaking process. The primary objective of the reform was create institutionally unified and functionally integrated sectoral institutions, because it was perceived that government ministries' jurisidictional boundaries did not reflect newly emerging business realities. This mismatch occasionally brought about institutional inefficiencies and policy gridlocks as the Korean government could not make critical policymaking in a coherent and timely manner. The unified and integrated institutional structure resulted in substantially reducing the institutional transaction costs.

5.3 Institutional Transformation in the IT Industry

In making institutional transformation, the Korean government placed a high priority on recrafting a close relationship with the private sector rather than scrapping it. It was obvious that although the Korean government tried to create a new regulatory governance distinct from the existing model of developmentalism, it does not necessarily imply that it would replace informal regulatory governance forged in developmentalism with formal regulatory institutions under neoliberalism (Rhee 2014). While distancing away the orthodox developmentalism, the Korean government thought collaboration between public and private actors essential in upgrading the IT industry. The cozy relationship among stakeholders was important in promoting the IT industry. In contrast to the previous mode of industrial promotion that had relied on direct support and protection, it was necessary to develop a subtle and sophisticated governance that could enhance collaboration among stakeholders without overarching intervention by the government. For this goal, it was necessary to build an eco-system where major stakeholders such as government ministries, universities, research institutes, and private companies could communicate and cooperate with other (Song 2009). It was a clear departure from the past model of development in the sense that it was not the hierarchical system with the government at the apex but a horizontal system where major stakeholders could cooperate on an equal footing. Nonetheless, the new mode of development in the IT industry was a government-led discretionary liberalization. It was the Korean government that made major decisions, such as how many entrants to allow and how strong these entrants had to become to effectively compete with the vertically integrated dominant incumbent carrier.

Also, in terms of the degree of political intervention, the liberalization process in Korea was relatively depoliticized. Although some major decisions were subject to mediation by top leadership, intervention by politicians and various interest groups with keen interests in the IT industry remained minimal. This provided institutional capacity for the MIC to take an initiative in the liberalization process. It does not, however, imply that liberalization in Korea was free from political intervention. As demonstrated in the decision to designate SK as a second mobile service provider and LG's takeover of DACOM, the liberalization process in Korea was politicized in the various stages of liberalization (*Solidarity for Economic Reform* May 13, 1999).[1] Rather, even when the

[1] Arguing that LG's takeover of DACOM was a compensatory reward in return for LG's disposal of the semiconductor division, the Solidarity for Economic Reform heavily criticized the Korean government that the government implicitly connived *chaebol* expansion (Solidarity for Economic Reform May 13, 1999).

liberalization process was subject to politicization, the final outcomes still did not deviate from those envisioned by the MIC. In most cases, the MIC was able to impose its policy preferences on the courses of liberalization (Lee 2004).

While the ideological shift signaled an abrupt departure from the developmentalism of the past decades, it did not lead to a fundamental breakup of the Korean developmental state into the Anglo-American style regulatory state. The Korean liberalization process was completed by the Korean state's new activist role (Weiss 1998). To play the activist role, the Korean state thought that it was critical to create a highly unified institutional structure in the IT industry because the Korean government experienced various problems stemming from fragmented policymaking structure.

Meanwhile, the Korean government had to reduce uncertainties in the process of reformulating institutional foundations of the development state. Although the Korean government successfully guided industrial upgrading from labor intensive industries to heavy chemical industries in the 1970s, industrial upgrading to the IT industry posed daunting challenges. During the catch-up period, Korea as a late developer was content with replicating an advanced foreign model in an effective manner (Amsden 1989). While the fast follower strategy was still at work in some segment of the IT industry, it was generally believed that the overall efficacy of the catch-up strategy sharply declined. As Korea reached technological frontier, the foreign model to replicate was not simply available. In order to sustain economic development, the Korean government shared an understanding with the private sector that it was inevitable to actively embrace liberalization unleashed from the forces of globalization. The Korean government found that it was about time to shift from a fast-follower strategy to an industry-leading innovator strategy in developing the IT industry (Kim 2012).

Despite general consensus, it was not easy to mold a new institutional foundation that can be better fitted to the new era of development (Shin and Chang 2003). Foremost, unlike the previous stage of industrial development, it was virtually impossible to figure out whether one specific policy, either industrial promotion or protective measures, can be effective in developing the IT industry, because the complexity has dramatically increased in the IT industry. Although scholars have engaged in intense debates about the efficacy of industrial policy, it is difficult to verify whether one industrial policy produced positive or negative effects on industrial success (Noble 1989). It suggests that institutional foundations underlying industrial development is more important than a specific industrial policy. Rather than executing specific policies, it was more urgent to modify the existing institutions so that they could adapt to changing environments.

It was clear that the development of the IT industry could not rely on the past practices of government-led industrialization, because the Korean government alone could not cope with uncertain realities without close collaboration with other key players. The industrial transition required a new combination of government-business relations, which involved high uncertainties. Recognizing this changing environment, in the 2000s, the Korean government made various efforts to build a widespread consensus with the private sector.

The first outcome came with the successful development of 3.5 generation wireless communications technology, Digital Multimedia Broadcasting (DMB) (Kim 2012). In order to provide systematic supports that could help IT companies leapfrog to emerge as a technological leader, the Korean government had to creatively reformulate institutional foundations of the IT industry. The institutional transition involved a very complex nature in the sense that it was neither simple reproduction nor complete destruction of the past institutions. Rather the Korean government decompose and recreate institutional elements of the past, while simultaneously incorporating new elements needed to refine the institutional foundations (Park 2015). Institutional transition that aimed to create tightly coupled institutions involves a great deal of uncertainties and risks (Shin and Chang 2003).

The Korean government, in particular the Ministry of Information Communication (MIC) led the institutional transition with the close consultation with the private sector.[2] While the Korean government could not dictate the entire process of the institutional change, it still played a critical role in inducing cooperation from all relevant players with potentially conflicting interests (Kim 2012).

The Korean government took the lead in technology development and standard-setting as well. Again, the Korean government's central objective was to coordinate diverse interests among the relevant player. On the one hand, the Korean government mobilized various financial resources to speed up the standard-setting process. On the other hand, it also created a cozy environment where government, private companies, and universities could collaborate to nurture technological capabilities (Song 2009). Since technology development was an uncharted area Korean companies had never entered and therefore was full of uncertainties, the Korean government provided financial as well as other incentives to reduce risks involved in it.

In order to deal with the situation, the Korean government took two strategies. First, the Korean government created the 'Informatization Promotion Fund' (IPF) to provide financial support to private companies. The fund was raised to provide assistance in the following asreas: informatization, advancement of IT industry, advancement of IT infrastructure, R&D. With this financial clout, the Korean government could target a variety of technology development such as IP/CP, multimedia, software, digital broadcasting, semiconductor, parts and components, information protection, and IT services (http://www.archives.go.kr/next/search/listSubjectDescription.do?id=002004). For example, the Korean government injected about USD 40 million in the development of DMB alone (Kim 2012). With risks reduced, manufacturing companies became more active in developing IT technologies as demonstrated in the fact that most major IT devices manufacturers could participate in developing technologies combining wireless communications and DMB.

[2] The MIC, a principal ministry responsible for IT policy planning and implementation, was abolished in February 2008. The Lee Myung-bak government broke up the MIC's jurisdictional tasks to other ministries and commissions such as the Ministry of Administration and Safety, the Ministry of Culture, Sports, and Tourism, the Ministry of Knowledge Economy, and the Korea Communications Commission.

Second, the MIC utilized research organizations under government control as a platform where both public and private sectors could collaborate. The Electronic and Telecommunication Research Institute (ETRI) was a prime example that served as a coordinator between public and private sectors (ETRI 2002). It was not an easy task to encourage private companies to collaborate for technology development because manufacturing companies, mostly *chaebol* companies, were potential competitors. If not properly dealt with, the R&D platform could not escape the classic problem of free riding (Noble 1999). In order to overcome this problem, the ETRI made it clear that the public-private R&D consortium primarily focused on development of prototype technologies instead of commercial technologies.

This approach produced both intended and unintended outcomes. Foremost, private companies could rapidly develop technological capabilities. Beginning with the successful commercialization of CDMA technology, Korean IT manufacturers could emerge as a technology innovator. Also, many private companies were spun off from the R&D consortium, strengthening the eco-system of the IT industry (Seong 2003). In the past, the process of condensed industrialization created somewhat negative consequences. The concentration of economic power mainly into chaebol companies was one example. While this problem was raised in the context of social justice, it also created a problem in terms of unbalanced growth between *chaebols* and small-medium sized companies. In this sense, the spinning off of IT companies could potentially produce a sustainable industrial environment.

The line of the thinking was that it was necessary to nurture domestic technologies before foreign companies would encroach the Korean IT market. The government capacity to dominate industrial development substantially declined because the private sector did not have to rely on government support and protection as in the past. Domestic companies that were content with hierarchical relations with the government gradually attempted to disentangle themselves from institutions of the past decade (Kang 2002). However, widespread presence of highly sophisticated and complicated relations among numerous players indicated that it was increasingly important to coordinate diverse interests, thereby inducing cooperation among them. This new development paradoxically amplified the government's role as a coordinator (Wong 2005). Declining capacity in terms of overwhelmingly dictating the private sector was not a main problem for the Korean government. Rather, it was more important to separate tightly coupled institutional elements of the past in an orderly manner and creatively mold them to address new challenges.[3]

Various scholars have engaged in debates of the past and future lineages of the Korean developmental state. Scholars of developmental state argue that the Korean government largely relied on either tight control on financial resources (Woo 1991) or outright discipline of private actors (Amsden 1989). Recent studies still in the tradition of development state tend to highlight that the Korean government showed some degree of adaptive capacity by shedding off policy tools that had been available to the government in the high growth period (Thurbon 2003). In this perspec-

[3] In this regard, Ó'Riain (2007) argues that 'over-embeddedness' was a primary challenge the Korean government had to deal with.

tive, while it is undeniable that the Korean model of development underwent numerous changes, these changes should be understood within the boundaries of path dependence.

However, those critical of the developmental state thesis argue that the Korean model of development, essentially a catch-up model, was outdated and thereby destined to fade away facing domestic and external challenges. In this view, the efficacy of the Korean model of development expired with a series of changes made in the aftermath of the Asian financial crisis (Pirie 2005).[4]

While both perspectives aptly point to strengths and weaknesses of the Korean development model, it falls short of explaining how the Korean model of development has evolved once the catch-up period was over. The case of the IT industry in Korea demonstrates that the Korean government successfully recrafted institutional foundations to adapt to rapidly changing environments. Although the Korean government was unable to wield power in controlling private players as in the past, it still played a critical role by re-creating tightly integrated institutions, effectively coordinating potentially opposing interests, and actively embracing the forces of globalization. This policy direction was not set by a private actor. Rather, the Korean government took an initiative in setting ambitious goals and delineated the roadmap to transform the industry from fast follower to first mover. In this regard, the development of the IT industry in Korea can hardly be explained without resorting to the role of the Korean government. And at the core was institutional reconfiguration led by the Korean government.

Under the reconfigured institutions, the Korean government could manage to coordinate diverse and potentially conflicting interests among various players and stakeholders. However, since 2000, a cozy relationship among actors who had maintained the collaborative relationships in the 1990s began to unravel in the Korean IT industry. For example, in 2001, the Ministry of Information and Communication (MIC) and service providers revealed conflicting views in adopting the third generation International Mobile Telecommunication (IMT-2000). While the MIC preferred the existing CDMA, some service providers insisted that W-CDMA would be technologically more viable. Growing conflicts among the actors is also found among government agencies as well. It is well known that the MIC and the Korean Broadcasting Commission (KBC) clashed about jurisdictional authority over the Internet Protocol Television (IPTV) and the Digital Multimedia Broadcasting (DMB). Furthermore, growing conflicts are also witnessed within the private sector as cable service companies, communication service companies, broadcasting service companies, and communication service companies had different views in beginning IPTV (Lee and Park 2010).

Meanwhile, despite the growing conflicts, major actors in the IT industry still preferred maintaining existing policy network rather than abandoning it. They attempted to coordinate differing views on technological development, market pro-

[4]Walter (2008) argues that although the Korean government made a number of changes in returning for the IMF bailout, these changes were essentially 'mock compliance' without producing fundamental reformulation of the Korean model of development.

jections and the provision of service within it. Policy network in the Korean IT industry sponsored by the Korean government primarily prompted major players not to seek profound changes but to maintain the status quo. Because emerging industries such as IT industry are full of diverse uncertainties, major players tend to address this problem by creating a cooperative policy network encompassing government and business. Once created, the policy network tends to work as a self-reinforcing mechanism because the sunk costs in policy network are substantial. In particular, increasing switching cost renders major players to prefer the existing policy network. That is, the cost of exiting the network is bigger than the cost of (Lee and Park 2010) maintaining the network. Under the circumstance, major players tend to stick with the existing status-quo rather than abolishing it.

5.4 Self-Reinforcing Mechanism of Policy Network in the IT Industry[5]

The success and failure of the IT industry in South Korea can be explained in terms of the dynamics of self-reinforcing mechanism. Policy network is composed of actors with shared interests and preferences on a certain policy area. From the perspective of neoinstitutionalism, technologies or institutions, once adopted, tend to enhance the internal strength over time, creating path-dependency (North 1990). Major actors in the Korean IT industry create policy network as a means to spread economic and social uncertainty that they are likely to face in promoting the IT industry. Both government and private actors may face various unforeseen obstacles such as high start-up costs, volatile market changes, competition for domestic and international standard setting, and the trajectory of technological development. Major actors see it necessary to develop a cooperative institutional arrangement to deal with these daunting challenges (Lee 2004).

With the creation of stable policy network the IT industry, major actors believe they could effectively alleviate strategic uncertainties, thereby taking a long term perspective in nurturing IT industry. The Korean IT industry made two strategic choices that are intertwined with each other: one for technology development in the manufacturing sector and another for the market expansion in the telecommunications service. First, major actors in the Korean IT industry closely collaborated to create a series of joint research consortia in which government-affiliated research institutes, research institutes from the private sector, and universities participated. Second, government and private actors also made concerted efforts to systematically link technological development and the market expansion of telecommunications service because the fate of technological development hinges on the successful commercial introduction of those technologies.

[5] This section draws on Lee and Park (2010).

A question arises because, despite their shared interests in reducing strategic uncertainties, major actors are not likely to bear the costs of collective action involved in creating such a policy network (Olson 1986). Several factors such as prospective long term return, learning effects, and switching cost can be pointed out that facilitated self-reinforcing mechanism. Rapid pace of technology development and the introduction of new services tend to result in constant mergers and acquisitions among companies. Under such volatile market environments, both government and private actors perceive the maintenance of the existing policy network in their interests, given that the switching cost to a new policy network is prohibitively high. In addition, the MIC with a unified jurisdictional authority over the IT industry actively encouraged private actors to stick to the existing policy network. As a result, despite potential conflicts and policy failure, major actors did not pursue an alternative policy network to depart from the existing one.

The influence of policy networks was manifested since the early 2000s. Although tensions in the MIC-led policy network have begun to intensify among major actors in the Korean IT industry, they tried to maintain the policy network. First of all, among government actors, the MIC found it critically important to firmly establish its sole jurisdiction over the IT industry in institutional terms, defying challenges from other government agencies such as the Ministry of Commerce, Industry and Energy (MOCIE),[6] the Ministry of Education, and the Ministry of Culture. In 2000, the MIC and MOCIE competed to claim the post-PC, ubiquitous robotics companion, and mobile communication under their respective jurisdiction. They also launched various IT-related technology development projects to claim their sole jurisdiction. The inter agency competition and overlapping regulatory policies ultimately led to policy failures.

Competition for IT technology development also intensified between the MIC and the Korean Broadcasting Commission (KBC) with the convergence of IT and broadcasting technologies. In unveiling the satellite DMB service, the two agencies clashed to clinch the dominant position (*Electronics News*, May 28 2003). The conflict between them quickly escalated because the technological convergence was expected to be a mega trend in the IT industry, not just in Korea but also on a global scale. Furthermore, conflicts between the MIC and the KBC spilled over into the private sector. The conflict was not resolved until the National Assembly stepped in to enact the Amendment of Broadcasting Law in 2004.

Second, the MIC and private actors began to reveal dissenting views on the future trajectory of the global telecommunication market and the international standards. In 2001, the disagreement became obvious in the introduction of the third generation mobile service, or the IMT-2000. In dealing with the MIC's revealed preference over the CDMA standard, private companies showed diametrically different responses. While Samsung Electronics and Hyundai Electronics supported the MIC, LG Electronics and other companies that had not participated in the TDX and the CDMA projects preferred W-CDMA standard (Kang et al. 2006: 94).

[6] The MCI was renamed the MOCIE.

Despite diverging interests, both public and private actors did not attempt to discard the existing IT policy network. The selection process of IMT-2000 service providers vividly offers a clue why private actors chose not to abandon the policy network. Facilities-based service industry experienced a series of restructuring process from 1994 to 2010. Only those companies that were initially in the policy network were invited to participate in the M&A process. By the time when IMT-2000 service was introduced in 1999, the entire IT service industry was reorganized into an industry structure dominated by the so-called Big Three: SK Telecom, KT and LG Telecom. The industrial structure was maintained throughout the 2000s. By remaining in the policy network, major actors could acquire opportunities to enter the newly emerging business areas (Song 2009: 169).

The case of IPTV service also shows the way in which self-reinforcing mechanism played out. In 2005, the MIC and the KBC once again clashed over IPTV service. Both government agencies repeatedly displayed dissenting views over the future direction of development of the IT industry. A series of conflicts between the MIC and the KBC caused the delay of beginning of IPTV service until the National Assembly passed the IPTV Enforcement Ordinance in 2007. As in the case of the IMT-2000, the conflict between government agencies resulted in disagreements among private actors. Conflicts over the IPTV service were particularly serious between the telecommunication service companies and cable-TV service companies. The battle between the telecommunication and cable-TV service companies transferred toward the conflicts between the MIC and the KBC. However, despite this intensifying conflict, major actors still preferred to maintain the policy network because it was too costly to switch to an alternative institutional arrangement. Despite its policy mistakes, the MIC could still assure private actors that it was in their interests in remaining in the current policy network.

5.5 Conclusion

Thus far, I examined how the IT industry has evolved in Korea. In the face of internal and external pressures since the 1980s, the Korean government creatively led the liberalization process in the 1990s. Despite the stellar performance in the 1990s, however, the Korean IT industry came to be riddled with conflicts and policy failures since 2000. But this new development did not lead to the dissolution of the IT policy network. Rather, major actors still preferred to remain in the existing policy network for two reasons. First, major actors found it too costly to create an alternative policy network to replace the existing one.

Second, major actors also that exclusion from the network could bring about negative impacts on their future business. A series of restructuring of the IT industry shows that those who were in the policy network were repeatedly invited to participate in the emerging businesses of the IT industry.

References

Amsden, Alice H. 1989. *Asia's next giant: South Korea and late industrialization*. New York: Oxford University Press.

Electronics and Telecommunication Research Institute. 2002. CDMA Technology Development and Industrial Success. Electronics and Telecommunication Research Institute (in Korean).

Electronics News. 2003. May 28 (in Korean).

Evans, Peter B. 1995. *Embedded autonomy: States and industrial transformation*. Princeton: Princeton University Press.

Kang, David C. 2002. *Crony capitalism corruption and development in South Korea and the Philippines*. Cambridge: Cambridge University Press.

Kang, Ha Yeon, et al. 2006. *Interest mediation mechanism in the IT industry and trade policymaking*. Seoul: Korea Information Society Development Institute (in Korean).

Kim, Sung-Young. 2012. Transitioning from fast-follower to innovator: The institutional foundations of the Korean telecommunications sector. *Review of International Political Economy* 19 (1): 140–168.

Lee, Seungjoo. 2004. Transforming the Developmental State in Korea under Globalization. In *Handbook of Development Policy Studies*, ed. Gedeon M. Mudacumura and M. Shamsul Haque, 509–522. New York: Marcel Dekker.

Lee, Seungjoo, and Hyun Park. 2010. Self-reinforcing mechanism and continuity in policy network: The case of the Korean IT industry. *Review of Korean Political Science* 19 (3): 77–104.

MacIntyre, Andrew, T.J. Pempel, and John Ravenhill, eds. 2008. *Crisis as catalyst: Asia's dynamic political economy*. Ithaca: Cornell University Press.

Milner, Helen. 1988. *Resisting protectionism: Global industries and the politics of international trade*. Princeton: Princeton University Press.

Ministry of Information and Communication. 2003. *White paper on information and communication*. Seoul: Ministry of Information and Communication.

National Archives. Informatization Promotion Fund Projects. http://www.archives.go.kr/next/search/listSubjectDescription.do?id=002004.

Noble, Gregory W. 1989. The Japanese industrial policy debate. In *Pacific dynamics: The international politics of industrial change*, ed. Stephan Haggard and Chung-in Moon. Boulder: Westview Press.

Noble, Gregory W. 1999. *Collective action in East Asia: How ruling parties shape industrial policy*. Ithaca: Cornell University Press.

Olson, Mancur. 1986. A theory of the incentives facing political organizations. *International Political Science Review* 7 (2): 165–189.

Ó'Riain, S. 2007. *The politics of high tech growth: Developmental network states in the global economy*. Cambridge: Cambridge University Press.

Park, Sang Young. 2015. Analysis on the cohabitation of Developmentalism and neoliberalism in Korea: Changes in the Korean developmental state since the 1990s and varieties of developmental-neoliberal mixes. *Journal of Asia Pacific Studies* 22 (4): 5–40 (in Korean).

Pirie, Iain. 2005. Better by design: Korea's neoliberal economy. *The Pacific Review 18*(3): 355–374.

Rhee, Jong-Chan. 2014. Limits of Regulatory Governance Change in the Post-Developmental State: Korean Telecommunications Market Restructurings from a Comparative Perspective. *Asian Journal of Political Science* 24 (1): 142–161.

Rogowski, Ronald. 1990. *Commerce and coalitions: How trade affects domestic political alignments*. Princeton: Princeton University Press.

Shin, Jang-Sup & Ha-Joon Chang. 2003. *Restructuring Korea Inc*. Routledge Curzon.

Seong, Jiun. 2003. Policy evolution of information and communication liberalization. *Korean Public Administration Review* 37 (2): 333–353.

Solidarity for Economic Reform. 1999. On Chaebol's Takeover of DACOM and Korea Heavy Industry. May 13. http://ser.or.kr/bbs/board.php?bo_table=B11&wr_id=429&sst=wr_datetime&sod=asc&sop=and&page=9.

Song, Kyeong Jae. 2009. Policy networks and policymaking in the Korean IT industry. *The Korean Journal of Public Administration* 18 (3): 159–181 (in Korean).

Thurbon, Elizabeth. 2001. Two paths to financial liberalization: South Korea and Taiwan. *The Pacific Review* 14 (2): 241–267.

Yeung, Henry Wai-chung. 2014. Governing the market in a globalizing era: Developmental states, global production networks and inter-firm dynamics in East Asia. *Review of International Political Economy* 21 (1): 70–101.

Walter, Andrew. 2008. *Governing finance: East Asia's adoption of international standards*. Ithaca: Cornell University Press.

Weiss, Linda. 1998. *The myth of the powerless state*. Ithaca: Cornell University Press.

Weiss, Linda. 2000. Developmental states in transition: adapting, dismantling, innovating, not 'normalizing'. *The Pacific Review* 13 (1): 21–55.

Woo, Jung-en. 1991. *Race to the swift: State and finance in Korean industrialization*. Columbia University Press.

Wong, Joseph. 2005. Re-making the developmental state in Taiwan: The challenges of biotechnology. *International Political Science Review* 26 (2): 169–191.

Chapter 6
Restructuring and Continuity in the Aircraft Industry

6.1 Brief Historical Overview: The Quest for Industrial Upgrading

Until 1960s, Korea primarily concentrated on improving the maintenance capability of military aircrafts, starting with the overhaul maintenance of the L-19 reconnaissance aircraft in 1955 (Korea Aerospace Industries Association 2015). The Korean aircraft industry entered a new stage in the mid-1970s when it first began to seek coproduction. In the early 1970s, facing increasing security threat from North Korea, the Park government started internal discussions to examine the feasibility of indigenous development of aircrafts to improve self-reliant defense capability. The Park government carried out the modernization program of aircrafts in accordance with the "First Force Improvement Plan" to replace obsolescent F-5A and F-86. The Park Chung Hee government sought the coproduction of the "First F-X project" in order to modernize the defense capability of the Korean Air Force. While proceeding to acquire F-16, the Park government cautiously probed the possibility of coproduction. While the Park government attempted to coproduce both F-16 and F-5E/F, it could run the coproduction project of F-5E/F because the Jimmy Carter administration attempted to control arms transfer (Nolan 1986: 30–31).[1] Although the Park government's attempt was half-successful, it reflected the Korean government's long-term goal of enhancing indigenous capability of the defense-related industries (Um 2016).

From this period, the Korean government began to play a guiding role in industrial development of key sectors. In 1978, for example, with the enactment of the

[1] The Korean government skillfully took advantage of off-set programs in the purchase of foreign aircrafts as a means to enhance its R&D capabilities. In purchasing KF-16, for example, the Korean government could use off-set programs to improve manufacturing capacities for forward fuselage (Cho 2000).

S. Lee and S. Rhyu, *The Political Economy of Change and Continuity in Korea*,
The Political Economy of the Asia Pacific, https://doi.org/10.1007/978-3-319-71453-0_6

Aircraft Industry Promotion Act, the Korean government promoted the aircraft industry by designing and executing industrial policy such as provision of subsidies and incentives to attract foreign investment (Choi 2011). In the 1980s, Korea also entered into commercial aircrafts to produce parts for commercial aircraft manufacturers with Boeing and Northrop.

Despite improvement in its indigenous capability, the Korean aircraft industry could not escape from the structural problems of limited domestic demand. It created a fundamental problems such as weak production base, inability to achieve economies of scale, insufficient research and development capacities (Cho 2000). As the Korean aircraft industry failed to secure follow-up orders, idle capacity emerged as a major obstacle to accumulation of technologies and experiences since the mid-1980s. Therefore, the Korean aircraft industry largely remained in low-value added production of components and parts to become a Boeing subcontractor for assembly production of civilian aircraft components.[2] The Korean aircraft industry could not grow out of the stage of license production and maintenance that in turn retarded autonomous development capability.

In the 1990s, aerospace companies in Korea produced a variety of aircrafts under license to deliver to the Korean military. Korea started license production of F-16 and UH-60 helicopter. Korean Air and Samsung Aerospace produced UH-60P (Blackhawk) helicopters and KF-16 fighters with license agreements with Sikorsky and Lockheed Martin, respectively (Korea Aerospace Industries Association 2015). The KAI collaborates with Lockheed Martin to win T-X Project of the United States by to developing the advanced T-50A, or a variant of the T-50 trainer (Korea Aerospace Industries Association 2016). In the process, Korea succeeded in local production of fuselage. Despite the progress, the Korean aircraft industry ranked around 20th in the world and is behind other countries such as Spain and Brazil.

Although the Korea government enacted Basic Law for Aircraft Industry Promotion, it could not design the systematic strategies to promote the industry and make institutional arrangements to facilitate the development of the aircraft industry. Under the circumstance, the Korean government did not forge the dense networks among the government-affiliated research institutes, universities, and private companies that could advance the R&D capacities. Recognizing the problem, the Korean government once again enacted the law for the promotion of aircraft industry, but it did not lead to meaningful changes (Cho 2000). One reason was that the Korean government did not understand the subtle difference between research and development in the aircraft industry (Cho 2003).

The aircraft industry sought to offset the problems associated with limited domestic demand through exports as well as actively engaged in sales of aircraft to the commercial sector. As a result, exports increased by an annual average of 33.4% from the period of 1988 to 1992. During this period, order value, a leading indicator of exports, also recorded an average annual increase of 26.5%. Later, Korea began

[2] For the concise summary of the development history of the Korean aircraft industry, see Cho 2003 and Korean Association of Aircraft Industry 2015.

development of indigenous aircraft with the ADD's development of the KT-1 trainer and acquired jet plane technology through KAI's development of the T-50 advanced trainer (Korea Aerospace Industry Association 2015).

6.2 The Asian Financial Crisis and the Restructuring of the Aircraft Industry

Since the 1990s, Korea began to pursue an indigenous development of the aircraft industry, departing from the previous era that had primarily been limited to license production.[3] In the aftermath of the Asian financial crisis, the Korean government had to restructure not just the aircraft industry, but substantial structural changes of the Korean economy. While embarking on short-term measures to fight off the crisis, the Korean government also designed and implemented structural and institutional reforms.[4] The Korean political economy made profound changes in terms of industrial promotion, regulatory orientations, government-business relations, and institutional reconfiguration of the economic system. Under the mounting pressure from the government and activist NGOs, *chaebols* were forced to carry out profound restructuring programs in addition to corporate governance reform. The gist of the restructuring programs was address excess capacities in manufacturing sectors (The Publishing Committee of the Sixty-Year of the Korean Economy 2010).

The aircraft industry also went through the painful restructuring process. The aircraft companies particularly suffered from investment decline and increase in royalty payment. Cancellation of new contracts and scale-down of existing businesses exacerbated the difficulty to the companies, creating a problem of idling facilities. Given that the aircraft industry heavily relied on government procurement, the financial constraints of the Korean government severely restricted a systematic promotion of the industry. The decline in defense budget of the Korean government further exacerbated the difficulty. It is against this backdrop that the aircraft industry was pinpointed as a candidate for restructuring.

Because private companies could not develop production specialization among themselves, they suffered from excessive competition. As a consequence, four private companies specializing in fuselage assembly faced a problem of overlapping investment, becoming the obstacle to the systematic development of the industry (Lee 1998). In addition, the Korean aircraft industry faced a difficult time in enhancing domestic production ratio and technology acquisition because subcontractors did not develop to the extent which they could effectively support four major companies. In contrast to European countries such as France, the UK, and Germany that had just one aircraft manufacturing company, Korea had four companies with lim-

[3] Cho assesses that the current status of the Korean aircraft industry reached the stage between international cooperative development phase and independent development phase (Cho 2000).

[4] For a comprehensive overview of the structural reform after the crisis, see Shin and Chang (2003).

ited production differentiation among them, ultimately causing overlapping investment and excessive competition.

Because the technologies that Korea acquired from the license production is concentrated in the areas of fuselage and simple assembly, the Korean aircraft industry still lacked the high value-added system integration capability. In addition, the Korean government could not establish effective policy guidelines because it lacked the overall capacity to coordinate projects run by ministries. Close collaboration among various players is essential in development of the aircraft industry as multiple players are involved in the industry. The jurisdictional structure in the aircraft industry was highly complex and overlapping, often leading to ministerial conflicts rather than cooperation. Government actors in the Korean aircraft industry were the Ministry of Finance and Strategy, the Ministry of Industry, Trade, and Energy (MOITE), the Ministry of National Defense (MND), the Ministry of Science, ICT, and Future Planning (MOSIF), and the Ministry of Land, Infrastructure, and Transport (MOLIT). Among them, close collaboration between the MOITE, the MOLIT, the MOSIF, and the MND is particularly essential, because they were in charge of R&D, production, and procurement. However, these ministries did not possess coordinating capacities to oversee the development of the aircraft industry, creating problems of inefficiency and waste of scarce resources. For example, the institutional incapacities resulted in limited technological spin-off from defense sectors, although the aircraft industry heavily relied upon defense contracts for the majority of their revenues (Shin Dong-A 2010).

The outbreak of the Asian financial crisis also turned around the dynamics of competition between Hyundai and Samsung. The direct cause was that Hyundai withdrew from the aerospace industry. Because throughout the 1990s, private companies had to provide a matching fund to join the projects initiated by the government (Kim 2006), the private companies that had suffered from serious liquidity problems in the wake of the crisis were unable to sustain aircraft business. Although other companies such as Samsung remained in the aircraft business, they also experienced serious deterioration of profitability.

Against this backdrop, the Korean government took an initiative in restructuring of the aircraft industry in the wake of the financial crisis. In October 1999, Daewoo Heavy Industries (now Doosan Infracore), Samsung Techwin (now Hanhwa Techwin), and Hyundai Aerospace merged into the KAI, which emerged as a sole aircraft manufacturer in Korea (Ahn 2012). The three companies could increase capital by 33.4 billion won because creditors such as Korea Development Bank and Woori Bank agreed to a debt for equity swap.[5] The Korean government played a central role in managing the overall M&A process. To facilitate the

[5] Nonetheless, the restructuring process was full of uncertainties and conflicts. The aircraft engine division of Samsung and aerospace manufacturing division of the KAL did not participate in the KAI to seek independent survival. In particular, the KAL was adamantly opposed to the merger, arguing that it was unreasonable to merge with the three companies in trouble.

merger, the government also injected financial resources into the KAI by placing an additional order for 20 units of F16 (*Dong-A Daily* September 22, 2000).[6]

The government's plan to promote the aerospace industry began to materialize in 1999 with the enactment of the Basic Plan for the Development of the Aerospace Industry ("Basic Plan for the Aircraft Industry Development" <https://www.kari.re.kr/kor/sub04_02_01.do>). In accordance with the government initiative, major companies aspired to transform into a system integrator. This attempt was initially made in satellite division, as major companies accumulated technologies and experiences as a sub-system producer by the mid-1990s. Before the Asian financial crisis, Hyundai Electronics and Samsung Aerospace Industries intensely competed to establish themselves as a sole system integrator in Korea because the system integrator could secure the majority of government contracts.

The two companies' strategy to transform into a systems integrator was profoundly different. Hyundai attempted to be a system integrator by participating in the development of commercial satellites. Unlike other Korean aerospace companies that had joined international joint development projects that primarily supplied components related to communications, Hyundai directly participated in satellite manufacturing. By acquiring technological capacities to develop satellites, Hyundai aspired to become a sole systems integrator in the Korean aerospace industry. By contrast, Samsung Aerospace Industries placed a higher priority in the domestic market by actively participating in various development projects as a provider of subsystems. Based upon these experiences, Samsung tried to emerge as a systems integrator, although the Korean government turned down its plan for independent development of satellites.

The merger process continued in the 2000s because the Korean government made it clear from the beginning that it would privatize the KAI once it consolidated the industrial structure in the aircraft industry. The Korean government thought that it was necessary to privatize the KAI to prevent the problem of lax management joint. However, the creation of the KAI de facto set an entry barrier against other companies in the aerospace industry such as the KAL. In 2003, the KAL that had not participated in the merger process attempted to take over Daewoo's share in the KAI. Facing slump in commercial division, the KAL tried to amplify the synergy between defense and commercial businesses. It was Doosan Infracore, not the KAL that became a shareholder of the KAI in 2004, as it took over Daewoo Heavy Industries and Machinery (*Chosun Daily*, August 5, 2004).

After establishing the KAI, the Korean government actively promoted the aircraft industry in the 2000s. The Aerospace Industry Promotion Act, revised in April 2009, stipulates that the Korean government can designate a special business provider to enhance research and development of the aerospace industry by offering preferential loans (Aerospace Industry Development Promotion Act 2009). Following on this, in 2009, the Korean government once again announced that it

[6] Experts were highly critical of the move made by the government: they thought that the Korean government unduly backed the KAI that was created by the government initiative, violating market principles.

would seek the privatization of the KAI by selling off stocks held by the Korea Development Bank, or the biggest shareholder of the KAI.[7] In 2015, the Financial Reform Commission suggested the KDB to sell the stakes in ninety one non-financial corporations by 2018 (*Chosun Biz* April 4, 2016). The KAL consistently pushed for the takeover of the KAI in order to address the aggravating business environment.[8] Assessing that the KAL did not have potential to grow into an internationally competitive system integrator, however, the Korean government reversed its position to maintain the existing industrial structure led by the KAI.

Under the circumstance, in May 2016, the KDB decided to transfer some of its share, about 7.54 million share, to the Korea Exim Bank in the form of investment in kind. The objective of the decision was two-folded. On the one hand, the KDB in coordination with the government's position thought that the aircraft industry should maintain the current industrial structure until the KAI is fully privatized rather than selling off part of the share. On the other hand, the KDB aimed to strengthen the capital soundness of the Korea Exim Bank (*Business Post*, May 20, 2016).[9] The Korea Development Bank as a major shareholder that owns 26.7% of KAI stocks planned to privatize the KAI. Hanwha Techwin with 4.99% share of the KAI was initially regarded as a promising candidate interested in take-over of the KAI. However, the privatization of the KAI delayed as Hanwha Techwin divested about half of its 10% shares in the KAI (*Korean Economic Daily* 1/11/2016).[10] The privatization was further delayed as Doosan sold out its stakes of the KAI.

6.3 Between Indigenous Development and International Collaboration

While carrying out the restructuring of the aircraft industry, the Korean government attempted to resurrect the plan to nurture indigenous capabilities. The Korean government made continuous efforts to develop indigenous aircraft started with the Korean Fighter Program (KFP), dating back to the late 1980s. In the 1990s, the Korean government pushed for indigenous development of *Chang-Kong* 91 and KTX-1 (Cho 2003). These plans envisioned dual objectives of strengthening the air force through acquisition of a main fighter aircraft, while boosting the domestic aircraft industry. Although it was far more expensive (about $1 billion) than direct purchase from the original manufacturer, the program was purposely structured for

[7] In 2006, the Korea Development Bank (KDB) became the major investor by injecting 210 billion won into the KAI. In 2009, the KDB possessed 30.5% of the KAI's share.

[8] Since the establishment of the KAI, the KAL was in trouble in expanding its business into defense sector.

[9] It is equivalent to about 500 billion won.

[10] It was reported that Hanwha Techwin decided to expand the engine component business by pursuing overseas M&As instead of taking over the KAI (*The Korea Herald* January 6, 2016)

production of the F-16 aircrafts under license in Korea.[11] It was expected to provide the Korean aircraft companies with an opportunity to acquire technologies required for development and production.

The acquisition of R&D and technological capacities gained from the production of military aircrafts, albeit limited, served as a stepping stone for the development of more advanced military aircrafts (Cho 2000). Building on the production experience gained from license production the UH-60 helicopter program and KF-16 and enhanced research and technological capabilities by the government support, the Korean government began to examine the possibility of indigenous development of aircraft.

In 1997, in the Kim Young-sam government, the Ministry of Industry and Resources in collaboration with the Ministry of Finance and Economy, the Ministry of Defense, the Ministry of Construction, and the Ministry of Science and Technology took the lead in drawing up the draft version of the "Basic Plan for Aircraft and Aerospace Industry Development." Under the Basic Plan, the Korean government outlined "four strategies" to achieve the goal (Basic Plan for Aerospace Industry Development <https://www.kari.re.kr/kor/sub04_02_01.do>).:

1. Indigenous aircraft development for market and technology acquisition
2. Export promotion of core components and air market services
3. Increase in R&D efficiency
4. Advancement of industrial infrastructure

The goal designated by the Basic Plan was regarded essential to develop indigenous aircrafts. The Kim Young-sam government decided that Korea would complete the development of the next generation fighters by 2015. To implement the strategies set out by the government, the KAI drew up a new growth strategies: (1) Development of derivative models and expansion for domestic program; (2) Building up for commercial business and strengthening of a strategic partnership with global leading companies; (3) Exploring future programs as an OEM; (4) Strengthening of a development capacity with innovation of new technology. The KAI expects that it will become the top five companies in the aerospace industry as its annual revenue reaches USD20 billion by 2030 (http://www.koreaaero.com/english).[12]

The Korean government's plan to enhance indigenous capabilities of the aircraft industry continued in the 2000s. In 2010, the Ministry of Knowledge Economy (MKE) unveiled an ambitious "Aerospace Industry Primary Plan (2010–2019)" to boost aerospace industry's competitiveness. Under this plan, the MKE aimed to increase Korean aerospace industry's production capacity from USD 2 billion to

[11] It was a massive investment given that the total production amount of the domestic aircraft industry was just about U$200 million at that time.

[12] While Korea has nurtured aircraft industry for the last four decades, it has also imported commercial and defense aircrafts and their parts and components. In 2012, Korea imported about USD 3.8 billion. In 2014, the amount of import has increased to USD 4.05 billion. The US companies are the largest export to Korea as demonstrated in the fact that they accounted for about 40% of the Korea's entire import in 2014.

USD 20 billion in the period from 2009 to 2020. If completed as planned, the Korean government anticipated that the Korean aerospace industry would emerge as the 7th largest producer in the world. The plan once again aimed to nurture indigenous capabilities of domestic manufacturers in such areas as mid-sized fixed-wing commercial aircrafts, fighters and attack helicopters, UAVs, and core components and MRO services (The Ministry of Knowledge Economy 2010). The Korean government targeted the aerospace industry to substantially improve R&D capabilities to produce complete aircrafts, while importing core technologies, if necessary.

However, the plan did not proceed as expected. Rather, the government plan to develop indigenous aircrafts faced a serious setback. Despite the continuous efforts the Korean aircraft companies had a difficult time in obtaining core technologies in terms of fighter aircraft research and development. In order to overcome this imbroglio, the Korean government and aircraft industry turned to indigenously develop basic and advanced trainers. After the thorough review in 2006–2007, however, the Roh Moo-hyun government came to a conclusion that the mass production of the KFX was not feasible.[13] In November 2013, the Joint Chiefs of Staff made a final decision to purchase Lockheed Martin F-35A stealth fighters as Korea's next-generation fighter aircraft. While the Boeing F-15 SE was another candidate, the Korean Air Force preferred jet fighters with stealth capabilities (*Business Korea* September 25, 2013).[14]

In order to address this setback, the Korean government and the KAI shifted to development of T-50, the first supersonic trainer, which was launched in 1997. The KAI completed the full-scale development and earned first contract with the Korean Air Force in 2003.[15] Since its first delivery in December 2005, the Korean aircraft industry has made steady progress in developing military aircrafts such as the FA-50 and unmanned aerial vehicles (*Hangyeoreh* December 29, 2005). Encouraged by such development, it was anticipated that the aircraft industry would be able to increase exports by developing components, maintenance and repair industry, while it carries out R&D policies to develop core technologies.[16]

T-50/FA50's overall specifications and performance are quite advanced as it is highly weaponized compared to other competitors (Insinna 8/30/2016). While the T-50 is considered as the most advanced trainer, it was expensive for next generation pilot training. It was mainly due to high development cost, which was about 2.2 trillion won. Owing to T-50's expensive price, the KAI failed to win the bid four con-

[13] The review was based on the report by the Korea Development Institute that was critical of the KFX development.

[14] Korea planned to purchase forty F-35 in 2018 and may purchase additional twenty aircrafts, depending on the required operational capability.

[15] The Korean Air Force uses T-50 for advanced pilot training.

[16] The development of the space sector is relatively retarded compared to the aircraft sector, accounting for the about 10% of market share in the entire aerospace industry. To address the industrial setback, in 2016, the Korean government drew up the Mid-to-Long Term Space Development Plan which included a detailed development plan of the space industry. The plan specified that it was needed to build up KSLV-II (Korea Space Launch Vehicle- II) by 2020 to increase satellite exports, of which the prime goal is.

secutive times. The KAI could not acquire the contract with the United Arab Emirates, Singapore, Israel, and Poland, losing the bidding to Italy's M-346 (*Premium Chosun* April 12, 2014). In order to address this setback, the KAI made a bold decision to modify T-50 into a fighter, FA-50. The versatility of FA-50 that can be used both as light fighter and trainer greatly boosted its competitiveness both in terms of price and performance (*Chosun Daily* 4/12/2012).

An export contract of sixteen T-50s to Indonesia was a new momentum for the consistent development of T-50.[17] Since it earned the first export contract of 16 units of FA50 to Indonesia in 2011,[18] the KAI could win the export contract of 12 units to the Philippines in 2013, winning over JAS 39.[19] These export contract expedited the KAI's development of T-50. The Korean government helped the KAI develop the T-50 in two ways. First, for the export of the T-50, the Korean government helped the KAI by providing the government-to-government contract. With the support from the Korean government, the KAI could win the contract of FA-50 with Iraq worth $1.1 billion by making the PBL contract for maintenance for the next 25 years in December 2013 (Kim 2014). Second, the Korean government also assisted the KAI with the Defense Acquisition Program Administration, which helped the KAI secure orders and maintain production capacity without serious interruption. The Korean government also utilize DAPA to export military aircrafts, as demonstrated in the case of the joint development of KFX with Indonesia (Defense-Aerospace.com <http://www.defense-aerospace.com/article-view/release/158646/korea,-indonesia-advance-kf_x-fighter-project.html>. As a result, the total amount of the KAI's new order reached 7.2 trillion won by 2014[20]. The KAI's sales amount and profit increased by 20.1% and 23.5%. The breakdown of the production in the Korean aerospace industry is as follows: military aircraft 44%, commercial aircraft parts 32%, engine parts 7%, space projects 4%, and engine and fuselage maintenance 10% (Korean Aerospace Industries Association 2015: 4).[21]

The export of T/FA-50T, together with KT-1, contributed to the development of aircraft industry.[22] The production line-up of Korean aircraft companies has diversified. For the military aircrafts, Korea successfully developed and produced military helicopters, super-sonic trainers such as (T-50), and UAVs. In the military aircraft, T-50 and KUH (Korean Utility Helicopter: *Surion*) related production account for

[17] The KAI modified the T-50 into the FA-50, which is the light attack version of the T-50. The T-50 has several variants such as FA-50, T-50B (Advanced Maneuverability Aerobatic Plane) and TA-50 (Lead-in Fighter Trainer). The TA-50 is a variant equipped with a multi-mode radar, swing role capability of intercept and Close Air Support (CAS) and key A/A and A/G weapons (KAIA 2015).

[18] With this contract, Korea became sixth country to export a supersonic aircraft in the world.

[19] The contract amount was about 402 million US dollars (Parameswaran 2015).

[20] It includes 2 trillion won sales for civilian aircraft components with the Boeing and Airbus (Kim 2014).

[21] The number of T-50 produced by the KAI reached 200 units in 2015 ten years after it began to produce (*Korea Economic Daily* 9/8/2015).

[22] The KAI successfully completed the system development of T50 that had begun in 1997.

21% and 17%.[23] For commercial production, the KAI introduced a variety of indigenous aircrafts since having succeeded in developing the first Korean commercial aircraft, *Naraon* in 2008 (KAI <http://www.koreaaero.com/>). In this process, the Korean government played a pivotal role in creating the cooperative governance among government, manufacturers, and research institutes.[24]

However, it does not necessarily mean that the establishment of the KAI removed all the problems in the Korean aerospace industry. Despite structural changes, the Korean aerospace industry faced difficulty in securing financial resources in catching up with advanced countries. For example, R&D budget for aerospace industry should increase eight times to match the level of Japan's R&D resources (Park 2014). Under license production program, however, the Korean aircraft industry could merely acquire technologies through simple assembly such as fuselage assembly.

Owing to this problem, the Korean aircraft industry was divided over the issue of autonomous development or international collaboration. Although the Korean government ambitiously claimed to nurture the domestic industry, criticism against the government policy was raised that the lack of systematic management such as the recurrence of flood of small-medium sized enterprises and the subsequent restructuring created inefficiencies in the industry (*Shin Dong-A* 2011). For example, from 2011 to 2013, the KAI and the ADD proceeded an exploratory development ahead of system development. However, the KAI could start system development in December 2015 only after long delay of technology transfer from the US. Also, although the defense division dominates the Korean aircraft industry in terms of market share and production capacity, the technological spin-off to commercial business was limited. The Ministry of National Defense's preference over the US aircrafts further exacerbated the Korean aircraft industry's dependence on U.S. aerospace companies (*Shin Dong-A* 2011).

By contrast, the emphasis on indigenous development does not require the aircraft manufacturers to abandon international collaboration. Fully recognizing that sole dependence on international collaboration is unrealistic, proponents of autonomous development argued that without securing indigenous technological capabilities, the Korean aircraft industry would not be able to climb the industrial technological ladder, remaining in the low-value-added production in the industrial value chain.[25]

Meanwhile, the Korean government recognized the growth potential of the commercial division was increasingly important. Because the commercial demand for the industry rapidly increased in the 1990s, the Korean government had a view that

[23] The KF-X project, launched in 2015, will take up the substantial share as its development cost is expected to be about USD 8 billion (*Joongang Daily* 2016/1/22).

[24] For example, the Korean Aerospace Research Institute developed unmanned tilt-rotor aircraft to transfer to the Korean Air Line (KAL) for commercialization.

[25] At the global level, major players show a greater tendency to collaborate with foreign partners as risks and uncertainties have increased in various stages from R&D to production. They actively seek to form international collaboration to reduce the risks and uncertainties (Cho 2000).

it was time for the government to take the initiative in developing new technologies in order to collaborate with Boeing and Airbus as a risk sharing partner (Byun 2014: 59). Because indigenous development of large civilian airliners was not a viable option, the Korean government turned to international joint development, departing from its traditional emphasis on indigenous development. Furthermore, criticism was made that the excessive dependence on the defense division would dissipate the growth potential of the aircraft industry in the long term. The voice was growing that it is crucial to generate synergistic linkages between indigenous development and international collaboration (Yang 2008). The KAI became active in international collaboration to provide parts and components for with Boeing and Airbus, thinking that international collaboration would facilitate its advancement into the civilian sector. The Korean government also expected that this policy shift would be able to induce small and medium-sized enterprises' participation to nurture the aircraft industry's industrial development as well as defense capabilities of the Korean military. The shift to international collaboration was expected to create enormous industrial effects such as the establishment of about 300 companies and the creation of about 70,000 employment (KOTRA 2016).

In short, the Korean government and the KAI closely collaborated to diversify the business portfolio rather than exclusively pursuing indigenous development or international collaboration. In 2010, the Development Policy Commission of the Aerospace Industry, chaired by the Minister of Knowledge Economy, announced the Basic Plan of the Aerospace Industry. The plan was a comprehensive development strategy, linking military and commercial aircraft sectors, which aims to expand the production capacity from USD 1.9 billion in 2009 to USD 20 billion in 2020 (Choi et al. 2010: 4). The KAI also made contracts with the MOITE and the DAPA, signaling that the KAI attempted to establish a systematic linkage between commercial and military aircrafts from the development stage. Under the contract with the MOITE, the KAI will develop Light Civil Helicopter (LCH), while signing a contract with the DAPA to develop Light Armed Helicopter (LAH) (*Joongang Daily* 6/26/2015). The LCH and LAH will be designed to share 62% of components, which will reduce the development costs by 340 billion won as well as to lower operation and maintenance costs.[26]

Under the circumstance, the KAI maintained the dual strategy of indigenous development and international collaboration. First, the KAI continued to develop indigenous aircrafts such as the KFX, Light Armed Helicopter, and Surion-based helicopter variant, and UAV. The KFX plan is noteworthy, which is a program to develop the next generation fighter to replace decades-old F-4s and F-5s of the Korea Air Force.[27] In January 2016, the Defense Acquisition Program

[26]The development costs will be 650 billion won and 350 billion won, respectively. Domestic companies and Airbus Helicopter will share the development costs by investing 200 billion won and 400 billion won (*Joongang Daily* 6/26/2015).

[27]The KAI says that the development of the KFX will be completed by 2025 and the deployment will begin from 2032 (Kwaak 2015).

Administration (DAPA) and the KAI officially announced that they will launch the development of the KF-X program, which will proceed as long as 10 years. The total costs from development to production will amount to 18 trillion won. The KAI will produce one hundred twenty units by 2032. The KAI aims to increase localization ratio of the KF-X to 65% by developing as many as ninety items including AESA radar, mission computer, and Electro Optical TarGeting Pod (EO TGP) (*Global Defense News* 2015).[28] The Korean government was successful in making financial arrangements for the multi-billion-dollar project. While it provides 60% of the total production costs, the Korean government also secured 20% of the costs from the Indonesian government. The main developer KAI and its technology partner Lockheed Martin will provide the remaining 20% of the funding (Kwaak 2015).

Second, the KAI has strengthened international partnership with leading aircraft companies for commercial business. In the area of commercial aircraft, the KAI attempted to expand collaboration by making partnership to supply aerostructures to major aerospace manufacturers such as Boeing, Airbus, and Lockheed Martin. The KAI's strategy was based on the estimation that demand for commercial aircraft would steadily increase at least for a decade, because the combined order backlog of Boeing and Airbus was equivalent to about ten years' worth of deliveries (Yong 2017). Specifically, the KAI supplies fuselage and wing components for B747 and A380, aerostructures for F-15, and fuselage for AH-64D Apache attack helicopter. The KAI also produces B737 empennage, B777 FLE (Fixed Leading Edge), B787 PBH (Pivot Bulkhead) and wing and fuselage connection parts, A350 wing structures, and A320 wing top panels (Korean Aerospace Industries Association 2015).

While parts and components production takes up the majority in the commercial section, the KAI and the Korean Air also joined the upswing of supply chains of Boeing and Airbus. Emerging as a tier 1 partner for Boeing and Airbus, the KAI could participate in the process from design to production and delivery. The Korean Air that had mainly produced wing and fuselage structures could also participate in the development process of B787 and A350 as a global partner of Boeing and Airbus. The Korean Air with its own technology carries out design and development of the Airbus 350 cargo door and will manufacture sharklet wingtips for A330 ("Airbus Selects Korean Air Aerospace to manufacture Sharklet wingtips for the A330neo Family" 2015).[29] As a result, both companies account for 71% of the Korean aerospace industries' commercial exports for such projects as B777, B787, A320, and A350. About 36% of the export goes to the US, whereas the share of

[28] However, the development process will likely to face serious obstacles because the US government decided not to transfer four core technologies including Active Electronically Scanned Array (AESA) Radar (*Joongang Daily* 1/22/2016).

[29] The KAI was awarded by Boeing as the Supplier of the Year in 2010 and 2012 (KAIA 2015).

European countries such as France, the UK, and Germany is about 24% (Korean Aerospace Industries Association 2016).

It is noteworthy that Iraq, Japan and the Philippines emerged as a new destination for export of the Korean aerospace industry. The three countries accounted for 23%, 8%, and 5%, respectively (Korean Aerospace Industries Association 2016: 5). The KAI supplied parts and components to Japanese manufacturers such as Kawasaki Heavy Industries (KHI) that closely collaborate with Boeing. The KAI also succeeded in acquiring a contract with Airbus to supply wing bottom panel (Park 2014b). Thanks to the increase international cooperation with Boeing and Airbus, the total amount of production increased to USD5.73 billion (Korean Aerospace Industries Association 2016: 4).

6.4 Conclusion

The Asian financial crisis became a watershed in the Korean aircraft industry as it generated enormous pressures for restructuring. Far from relying on the market mechanism, the Korean government actively managed the restructuring process to create the KAI. The Korean government placed a policy priority on the harmonization of indigenous development and international collaboration rather than exclusive pursuit of either of the two. The Korean government came to a conclusion that the sole reliance on foreign companies without autonomous capacity would likely to retard the overall development of the aircraft industry. Based on this assessment, the Korean government in collaboration with the KAI took a balanced approach to indigenous development and international collaboration that contributed to the growth of the aircraft industry in Korea.

Nonetheless, the Korean aircraft industry faces daunting challenges ahead. It lacks system integration capability from design, test, and business maintenance to final assembly (Lee 1998). The Korean aircraft industry has gradually expanded the industrial base by developing unmanned aerial vehicles and attack helicopters. However, in 2008, Korea's aircraft industry accounted for merely 0.5% in the global market and still relies on import of core components and technologies. The fact that the share of defense production is more than 60% as of 2016 is another structural problem in the Korean aircraft industry (Korea Aerospace Industry Association 2016).[30]

It is in stark contrast to the market, where the ratio of military and commercial aircraft production is roughly 2–8. The Korean aircraft industry needs to increase the commercial production to reduce dependence on the defense sector that has substantially facilitated the take-off of the aircraft industry.

[30] In the case of the KAI, defense sector and civilian sector account for 67% and 33% of the KAI's sale, respectively (*Chosun Biz* April 4, 2016).

References

Aerospace Industry. http://www.export.gov/southkorea/doingbusinessinskorea/leadingsectors-forusexportsinvestment/aerospace/index.asp.

Aerospace Industry Development Promotion Act. 2009. <http://elaw.klri.re.kr/eng_service/lawView.do?hseq=17895&lang=ENG>.

Ahn, Seok-hyun. 2012. The Product of the 'IMF' Big Deal. *BizChosun*. September 27 (in Korean).

Airbus Selects Korean Air Aerospace to manufacture Sharklet wingtips for the A330neo Family. 2015. http://www.airbus.com/newsroom/pressreleases/en/2015/04/airbus-selects-korean-air-aerospace-to-manufacture-sharklet-wingtips-for-the-a330neo-family.html. April 23.

"Back to Square One Due to Rejection of F-15 SE." 2013. *Business Korea*. September 25.

Basic Plan for the Aircraft Industry Development. 1997. https://www.kari.re.kr/kor/sub04_02_01.do (in Korean).

Business Post. 2016. May 20.

Byun, Wanil. 2014. Current Status and Forecast of Domestic Aircraft Industry. *Current Industrial and Technological Trend in Aerospace* 12 (1): 59–67. (in Korean).

Cho, Myeong-Chin. 2003. *Restructuring of Korea's Defense Aerospace Industry: Challenges and Opportunities?* Paper 28. Bonn International Center for Conversion.

Cho, Tae Whan. 2000. Challenges in Research and Development for the Korean Aircraft Industry. In *Emerging Threats, Force Structures, and the Role of Air Power in Korea*, ed. Natalie W. Crawford and Ching-in Moon. Santa Monica: RAND Corporation.

Choi, Woo-young. 2011. The History and Current Status of the Korean Aircraft Industry. *Trends in the Aerospace Industry* 9 (1): 20–29 (in Korean).

Choi, Young Jin, In Kyu Lee, and Kyung Tae Lee. 2010. Analysis of 2010-2019 Plan for the Korean Aerospace Industry Development. *The Review of Aircraft Industry* 72: 1–21. (in Korean).

Chosun Biz. 2016. April 4.

"Daewoo Heavy and Machinery To Sell KAI Shares." 2004. *Chosun Daily*. August 5.

"Export of T-50 Soared as It Modified into Fighter." 2012. *Chosun Daily*. April 12 (in Korean).

"Hanwha Techwin cancels KAI takeover." 2016. *The Korea Herald*. January 6.

Insinna, Valerie. 2016. "US Air Force Closes in on Assessment of Lockheed's FA-50." *Defense News*. August 30. http://www.defensenews.com/articles/fa-50-air-force-lockheed-martin-crada-airworthiness-assessment-international-sales.

"KAI Produced 200 Units of T-50. 2015." *Korea Economic Daily*. September 18 (in Korean).

"KAI to Develop Military and Commercial Aircrafts Simultaneously." 2015. *Joongang Daily*. June 26 (in Korean).

Kim, Doo Hwan. 2006. Korea's Space Development Programme: Policy and Law. *Space Policy* 22 (1): 110–117.

Kim, Ik Sang. 2014. Korea Aerospace Industry (KAI): Going beyond the Limitation of Domestic Manufacturers. *Company Analysis*. HRI Research Center. March 31 (in Korean).

Korea Aerospace Industries Association. 2015. *Korea Aerospace Industry 2015*. Korea Aerospace Industries Association.

Korea Aerospace Industries Association. 2016. Korea Aerospace Industry 2016-2017. Korea Aerospace Industries Association.

"Korea to Complete Development of the KF-X in Ten Years." 2016. Joongang Daily. January 22 (in Korean).

Kotra. 2016. Korea's Leading Industries: Aerospace. KOTRA.

Kwaak, Jeyup S. 2015. "Korea Aerospace Industries preferred Bidder for New Fighter Jet: Deal is part of Korean Fighter Experimental project." *Wall Street Journal*. March 30.

Lee, Sung Won. 1998. Restructuring of the Aerospace Industry. *The National Economy*, March: 113–116.

Ministry of Industry and Resources. 2002. Press Release. August 29 (in Korean).

Nolan, Janne E. 1986. *Military Industry in Taiwan and South Korea*. London: Palgrave Macmillan.

Parameswaran, P. 2015. “Philippines Receives 2 New Fighter Jets from South Korea.” *The Diplomat*. December 1.
Park, Jiyoung. ed. 2014a. Space Technology Development: Effects on National Security and International Stability. Asan Report.
Park, Moo Hyun. 2014b. “The Growth of the KAI Will Continue for Ten Years.” Etrade. February 24 (in Korean).
“Project Fighter KF-X / IF-X Confirmed to Continue.” http://www.defense-aerospace.com/article-view/release/158646/korea,-indonesia-advance-kf_xfighter-project.html
“Red Light Turned on the Privatization of the KAI.” 2016. *Korean Economic Daily*. January 11 (in Korean).
Shin, Jang-Sup, and Ha-Joon Chang. 2003. *Restructuring Korea Inc*. Oxford: RoutledgeCurzon.
“Surge of T-50 Export wth the Modification into FA-50.” 2014. *Premium Chosun*. April 12.
The KAI Delivered the First T-50. 2005. *Hangyeoreh*. December 29 (in Korean).
The KAI Signed a Contract for the KF-X. 2015. *Global Defense News*. December 29 (in Korean).
The KAI Will Produce 20 F-16 under License. 2000. *Dong-A Daily*. September 22 (in Korean).
The Ministry of Knowledge Economy. 2010. Press Release: The Roadmap of the Korean Aircraft Industry’s Leap (in Korean).
“The Ministry of Knowledge Economy that Calls for the Development of the Aircraft Industry, but Benefits the US Aircraft Companies.” 2011. *Shin Dong-A*. February 23 (in Korean).
The Ministry of Knowledge Economy that Feeds the US Aerospace Companies, while claiming the development of the Aircraft Industry. 2010. *Shin Donga-A*. March.
The Publishing Committee of the Sixty-Year of the Korean Economy. 2010. *The Korean Economy: Six Decades of Growth and Development*. Seoul: KDI (in Korean).
Um, Jungsik. 2016. Park Chung Hee Administration’s Fighter Experimental (F-X) Project and Carter Administration’s Arms Transfer Policy. *The Korean Journal of International Studies* 56 (1): 111–142. (in Korean).
Yang, Yong-Seok. 2008. Policy Recommendations for International Joint Development of Civilian Aircrafts. *Aviation Promotion* 47: 177–200. (in Korean).
Yong, Paul. 2017. “Aircraft Leasing.” *Asian Insights SparX-Aviation*. February 10.

Chapter 7
Dynamics of Policy Shift and Path Dependence in Foreign Economic Policy: Between Strategic Choices and Domestic Constraints

Since the late 1990s, East Asian countries have actively pursued free trade agreements (FTAs).[1] While it was a reaction to the rapid proliferation of FTAs in other regions, it was also East Asian countries' attempt to transform deepened economic integration among East Asian countries into more institutionalized arrangements (Aggarwal and Koo 2007; Pempel 2006). Korea was not an exception to this trend. As of July 2017, Korea has 15 FTA deals with 45 countries in effect, concluded an FTA with Central America, and negotiating four FTAs including the Korea-China-Japan FTA and Regional Comprehensive Economic Partnership (RCEP) (http://fta.go.kr/main/situation/kfta/ov/).

The FTA drive was essentially led by the Korean government. What prompted the Korean government to take the initiative in pursuing FTAs? Korea's shift to FTAs is puzzling in terms of both external and internal environments. As a country that had sought to integrate into the global economy, Korea was a consistent supporter of multilateralism centered around the GATT and the WTO. Since the late 1990s, however, Korea made a strategic policy change to promote FTAs as an important pillar of the foreign economic policy. It is often pointed out that the Asian financial crisis became a watershed in foreign economic policy of Korea. Running into the risk of reduction in global trade, Korea together with other East Asian countries was keenly aware that East Asian countries should strengthen not just economic ties but institutionalized cooperation in the region (Calder and Ye 2004). FTAs emerged as an alternative to effectively realize this policy goal.

From the domestic point of view, Korea's sudden shift to FTAs is also puzzling. Unlike conventional wisdom that understands trade liberalization as an outcome of the collective voices from the private sector, the Korean government played a cen-

[1] For economic and political dynamics of FTA expansion, see Baldwin (1993) and Ravenhill (2010).

S. Lee and S. Rhyu, *The Political Economy of Change and Continuity in Korea*,
The Political Economy of the Asia Pacific, https://doi.org/10.1007/978-3-319-71453-0_7

tral role in formulating FTA strategies. We shed light on the evolving path of Korea's FTA strategy since the late 1990s to demonstrate how and why the Korean government took the initiative even in the face of strong voice from the civil society (Lee 2010a). Furthermore, we examine why the Korean government that had actively pushed for FTAs under the domestic circumstance where strong opposition from agriculture and other politically sensitive sectors became cautious in shifting to mega FTAs.

7.1 The First Stage: Gradual Approach to FTAs

The Korean government took advantage of FTAs as a means to reformulate its traditional foreign economic policy. The Korean government's push for FTAs were primarily derived from its changing perception of FTAs' economic effects. Until mid-1990s, the Korean government was cautious in pushing for FTAs, because it believed that Korea as a trade dependent country would likely to benefit more from trade liberalization at the multilateral level. However, the proliferation of bilateral and minilateral FTAs in other regions encouraged the Korean government to reassess that FTAs would not necessarily be contradictory to multilateral trade liberalization.

Recognizing the increase in export as a viable policy option to cope with the liquidity trap during the Asian financial crisis, the Kim Dae-jung government came to a conclusion that Korea should jump on the worldwide trends of FTAs. Thinking that Korea should not be left behind in the FTA race any longer, the Korean government actively reformulated its foreign economic policy to incorporate FTAs. Rather than passively reacting to private sector's demand, the Korean government took the initiative in delineating Korea's new path to trade liberalization. It was not potential beneficiaries but the Korean government that shaped the contours of the new foreign economic policy.

Against this backdrop, the Kim Dae-jung government cautiously formulated its FTA strategies in terms of partner selection, speed, and scope. In November 1998 when Korea was still in the wake of the Asian financial crisis, the Korean government announced to embark on an FTA negotiation with Chile and established a special task force on a South Korea-Chile FTA, the Kim government also made a swift move to start feasibility studies with prospective FTA partners such as the United States, Japan, New Zealand, and Thailand (Sohn 2001: 7).

Despite the policy shift, the Kim government placed a high priority on reducing potentially negative economic effects of FTAs rather than seeking to maximize economic benefits. In particular, the Kim government was concerned about the opposition from the inefficient import-competing sectors. Market opening was formidable challenges, which may cause devastating impact for these sectors. Because the Korean government did not have institutional measures designed to salvage potential losers of trade liberalization, the Kim government was forced to take a gradual approach to FTAs.

The Kim Dae-jung government's approach was reflected in the selection of FTA partners (Yoo 2002). The Kim government chose geographically distant countries such as Chile as the first FTA partner. Chile ranked thirtieth among South Korea's trading partners, accounting for a mere 0.63% of its overall trade. Although Chile had a highly competitive and export-oriented agriculture, the Kim government thought that negative effects of agricultural liberalization was expected to be manageable due to seasonal difference between Chile and Korea (Yoo 2002). Singapore was also conceived as a good FTA candidate not just because it was eleventh trading partner (2.33%), but because it did not have competitive agricultural sector that had been traditionally protected from trade liberalization (KITA homepage www.kita.net). In a similar vein, the Kim government continued to select countries as a potential FTA partner with relatively weak economic ties such as India (sixteenth and 1.23%) and Canada (twenty-first and 1.11%) (KITA homepage www.kita.net).

7.2 The Second Stage: Global FTA Hub Strategy

While succeeding the Kim Dae-jung government's FTA strategy, the Roh Moo-hyun government turned more proactive in pushing for FTAs (Lee and Koo 2006). In contrast to the Kim government that conceived FTAs primarily as a trade strategy, the Roh government added strategic values to FTAs. In 2003, the Roh government drew up detailed FTA roadmap not just to increase economic gains but to realize its strategic goals (Lee 2007: 116; The Ministry of Foreign Affairs and Trade of Korea 2006).

The drastic changes in FTA strategy had to do with the Roh government's failure of its regional strategy. As demonstrated in its ambitious the Northeast Asia Cooperation Initiative (NEACI), the Roh government initially placed a high priority on Northeast Asia to promote regional cooperation. The Roh government anticipated that the era of Northeast Asia would form the community of prosperity by facilitating economic integration, which would ultimately contribute to the world prosperity (Sohn 2006). In this process, the Roh government expected that Korea would be able to emerge as a center of economic integration as well as a balancer in managing economic and security environment in the region in the region (Lee and Moon 2008).

Since 2004, however, the Roh government began to change its regional diplomacy as the NEACI initiative faced skepticism and severe criticism from domestic society and abroad (Kim 2008). The Roh government realized the harsh reality that the goal of joint prosperity could not lead to peace and confidence building in the region. As a result, the Roh government turned to new FTA policies. The rationale for this turnaround was that it was inevitable to pursue FTAs to fulfill the goal of "advanced trading state" (KIEP 2005).

The Roh government chose FTA policy as a means to realize a new regional strategy to gain competitive edge over other East Asian countries (Koo 2009).[2] The Roh government promoted FTAs as a primary foreign economic policy tool. The Roh government's renewed foreign economic policy was reflected into the FTA roadmap, which classified Korea's FTA partners into three groups: (1) immediate FTA partners such as Chile, Singapore, the EFTA, and Japan; (2) medium-term FTA partners such as Mexico, Canada, ASEAN, and China; and (3) long-term FTA partners such as the United States, the EU, and India. In accordance with this roadmap, in 2003, the Roh government's FTA strategy centered on simultaneous pursuit of FTAs and FTAs with major economies. First, the Roh government made clear that it would actively seek FTAs with as many countries as possible, departing from the Kim Dae-jung government's gradual approach. Second, despite increasing costs in pursuing multiple FTAs, the Roh government would pursue FTAs with major economies such as the US, the EU, and Japan in order to maximize the economic benefits rather than passively managing expected costs associated with FTAs (Lee 2010b).

Since then, the Roh government elevated the FTA strategy as an intrinsic pillar of Korea's foreign economic policy (Lee and Moon 2008). By unveiling a comprehensive roadmap for Korea's multitrack FTAs, the Roh government attempted to take advantage of FTAs to transform Korea as a global FTA hub (MOFAT 2006). It was a stark contrast to the previous Kim Dae-jung government where FTA strategy remained in the periphery.

While making swift moves in negotiating multiple FTAs simultaneously, the Roh government felt it necessary to conclude an FTA with major economies. Realizing that it was difficult to conclude the Korea-China-Japan FTA in the short term, in February 2006, the Roh government stunned the general public in Korea by turning to the Korea-US (KORUS) FTA. The decision reaffirmed that the Roh government took a proactive approach to FTA, fundamentally altering the Kim Dae-jung government's reactive strategy.

It was against this backdrop that the KORUS FTA emerged as a new alternative. The Roh government thought that the KORUS FTA would be essential to form not just the economic alliance but also the "comprehensive alliance" (Sohn and Koo 2011). The logic of comprehensive alliance was developed by both the Korean and US governments.[3] The Roh government asserted that the KORUS FTA would improve the bilateral relations that had been strained due to dissenting views about the North Korean nuclear issue and the relocation of the US military bases as well as would serve as a useful means to cope with strategic uncertainties that had rapidly increased with the rise of China and 9/11.

The opponents criticized that the KORUS FTA lacked policy consistency not just with NEACI initiative but with the "FTA Roadmap" designed by the Roh govern-

[2] For various discussions on FTAs as a foreign policy tool, see Higgott (2004), Capling (2008); Mochizuki (2009).

[3] For a concise overview of foreign economic policy as a means to enhance strategic interests, see Blackwell and Harris (2016).

ment. According to the initial FTA Roadmap, the Korean government was supposed to push for the KORUS FTA only after it concluded FTAs with Japan and China. They bitterly criticized that the Roh government suddenly reversed this sequence without offering any rationale (Kim 2008). In order to realize the initial policy goal of "economic hub of Northeast Asia," the Roh government should have sought FTAs in the order of the Korea-Japan FTA, the Korea-China FTA, the Korea-China-Japan FTA, and the East Asian FTA. However, the shift to the KORUS FTA ran counter to this vision (Lee 2006c).

Initially, the Roh government highlighted the economic benefits of the KORUS FTA to resort to the general public. President Roh stressed that the KORUS FTA would not just generate direct economic effects such as increase in GDP, trade surplus, and job creation, but also provide Korea with a chance to upgrade its economic structure. A successful KORUS FTA would most likely benefit South Korea's export industries such as automobiles and electronics, albeit at the expense of its less competitive agricultural and service sectors (Schott and Choi 2001).

Furthermore, Korea's deteriorating economic position in East Asia prompted the Roh government to seek FTAs with major economies outside the region. In the 2000s, South Korea's competitive advantage has seriously weakened as industrial structure of the three countries in Northeast Asia became competitive. The Roh government worried that South Korea's economic position would further weaken if China or Japan concluded an FTA with the US ahead of Korea (Moon and Rhyu 2010). The Roh government believed that the KORUS FTA had the potential to alter the dynamics of US-South Korean economic relations as well as the relations between the US, Japan, China, and South Korea.

However, the Roh government's strategy to focus on economic effects of the KORUS FTA did not work as expected.[4] Compared to other FTAs, the KORUS FTA was extremely controversial. Both governments made clear that they would seek comprehensive liberalization to make the KORUS FTA as the high quality FTA. It indicated that the Korean government would likely to face furious opposition from traditionally protected sectors including agriculture. Despite the emphasis on the equal relationship in the Korea-US bilateral alliance, the Roh government faced mounting pressure from a variety of interests groups such as agriculture, civil activist groups, and opposition parties. They argued that the Roh government betrayed again its supporters as it agreed to complete the negotiations of KORUS FTA within a year (Lee 2006b).

In particular, South Korea's uncompetitive sectors felt victimized by the Roh government's FTA initiatives and, more broadly, by its economic policies tilted toward neoliberalism. For those skeptics, the government's effort to restructure the economy by inviting external pressure, i.e. FTAs, would only worsen the issue of economic polarization in South Korea, rather than providing an opportunity to upgrade its economy to a more advanced level (Lee 2006c: 6). In contrast to their temporary disorganization during the Kim Dae-jung period, some of these veto players became more visible, as they began to work closely with anti-globalization

[4] For a US perspective on the KORUS FTA, see Feinberg (2003); Schott (2010).

NGOs and anti-capital labor unions.[5] It indicated that the explicit linkage of FTA policy to neoliberal reforms has galvanized industries and businesses that had slowly been recovering from the shadow of financial crisis (Lee 2006b).

This political situation further exacerbated in March 2006, a month before the launch of the KORUS FTA negotiations. A coalition was formed to bring together about 300 anti-KORUS FTA groups, thus becoming the largest coalition ever on a single policy issue during the Roh administration. Its core membership consists of agriculture and film industry that would most likely suffer from market liberalization. The ad-hoc coalition also included a number of progressive organizations such as the Korean Federation of Trade Unions, the Korean Teachers and Education Workers Union, and the Korean Federation of University Student Councils. These progressive groups rallied to protest against the KORUS FTA. It signified that the anti-KORUS FTA protests combined with an anti-American movement (*The Chosun Daily*, July 11, 2006).

In short, the assessment of the KORUS FTA was widely split among the general public in Korea. The pro-KORUS FTA camp asserted that given that the US is the only superpower and a longstanding ally, the strengthened alliance undergirded by the KORUS FTA would help Korea take the initiative in regional cooperation (Lee 2006a). In this view, "the KORUS FTA would lay the cornerstone to open a new era of the mature bilateral relations because it would provide both countries with a new material foundation to elevate the military alliance during the cold war period" (Koo 2006).

By contrast, skeptics of the KORUS FTA criticized that the Korean government leaning toward neoliberal ideas hastily pushed for reckless trade liberalization without paying due attention to the potential losers of the KORUS FTA. They further argued that even if economic gains are generated from the KORUS FTA, the gains will be concentrated on handful economic players such as *chaebols* and export-oriented sectors, rather than trickling down into the entire Korean economy (Lee 2006c).

7.3 The Third Stage: Linkage between Economy and Security

South Korea's entrance into the KORUS FTA negotiations signaled that the focus of its FTA policy profoundly changed from a reactive and gradualist strategy designed to minimize the negative effects of FTAs to a proactive and aggressive strategy aiming to maximize their benefits. The move toward the KORUS FTA illustrates the

[5] The Korean People's Action against FTA and WTO (KoPA) is a coalition of around 50 NGOs, social movement organizations, political parties, peasant organizations and trade unions. The coalition is designed to mobilize the disadvantaged groups and people to resist neoliberal globalization, while strengthening solidarity between different social movement groups (http://antiwto.jinbo.net/english/about.php).

Table 7.1 The KORUS negotiation process

Date	
2/2/2006	1st hearing held
2/3/2006	Negotiation announced
6/5/2006	Negotiation started
6/27/2006	2nd hearing held
4/2/2007	Negotiation concluded
6/21/2007	Supplementary negotiations continued
6/30/2007	Signed
9/7/2007	The KORUS bill presented to the 17th National Assembly
10/8/2008	The KORUS bill presented to the 18th National Assembly
4/22/2009	The KORUS bill passed in the Committee of Foreign Relations, Trade, and Unification of the National Assembly
12/3/2010	Supplementary negotiations concluded
2/10/2011	KORUS FTA Annex signed
5/4/2011	The KORUS bill withdrawn from the National Assembly
6/3/2011	The KORUS bill re-presented to the National Assembly
9/16/2011	The KORUS bill presented to the Committee of Foreign Relations, Trade, and Unification
11/22/2011	The KORUS bill passed in the National Assembly

Source: MOFAT FTA Homepage; http://www.fta.go.kr/new/ftakorea/kor_usa_daylist.asp?country_idx=19

proactive nature of Korea's FTA strategy led by the government. Realizing that it was not effective to stress economic benefits of the KORUS FTA, the Roh government attempted to securitize the KORUS FTA.[6] What then are the motivations for the Korean government to make such a choice?

The evolution of Korea's FTA strategy had to do with the domestic political landscape in Korea. While the Roh Moo-hyun government aimed to deepen economic integration through comprehensive liberalization by quickly concluding the KORUS FTA, it attempted to link economy and security in the face of mounting domestic pressure. As demonstrated in Table 7.1, the KORUS FTA was highly securitized as it went through the thorny process of negotiation, re-negotiation, and ratification process. The rationale was that the KORUS FTA would boost South Korea's economic as well as strategic position in East Asia (Koo 2006). The Roh government thought that the KORUS FTA would substantially improve the bilateral relations by transforming the bilateral security alliance into a more comprehensive one (Lee 2006a).

Such a change stemmed from the Roh government's understanding of the multi-faceted nature of the KORUS FTA. The Roh government thought that the KORUS FTA would contribute not just to upgrade economic system in Korea but to deepen economic ties between the two countries. Furthermore, the KORUS FTA would help the Roh government revitalize its vision of developing Korea as an East Asia's

[6] For various types of East Asian countries's linkage strategy, see Lee (2015).

economic hub. The KORUS FTA had the potential to alter the economic dynamics of U.S.-South Korean economic relations as well as the relations between the U.S., Japan, China, and South Korea. Based on the comprehensive alliance the Roh government anticipated that Korea could adapt to the rapidly changing security environment in Northeast Asia such as the rise of China, Japan's pursuit of normalization, and North Korea's nuclear ambition. In short, by shifting to the KORUS FTA, the Roh government aspired to achieve multiple goals – expediting domestic economic reforms to upgrade the Korean economy, developing Korea as a regional economic hub, and bolstering Korea's strategic interests.[7]

The Korean government's strategy to bring in security effects of the KORUS FTA re-emerged in the subsequent Lee Myung-bak government during the re-negotiation and ratification process. The Lee government created severe political and social confusion by agreeing to the US government's demand for re-negotiation. At the request of the Obama government, the Lee government agreed to re-negotiate the KORUS FTA to modify the initial agreement. In order to quickly complete the re-negotiation, the Lee government initially took the approach similar to that of the Roh government to highlight economic gains of the KORUS FTA. It claimed that with the conclusion of the KORUS FTA, "Korea's GDP would grow by 5.7% for the next 10 years, 350,000 jobs will be created, and annual trade surplus with the US will increase by $2.7 billion" (KIEP 2011). The Lee government also argued that the KORUS FTA, an FTA with the largest economic power in the world, would contribute to strengthen growth potential of the Korean economy, as it would expand trade, investment, and human interaction between the two countries (Press release by the Ministry of Strategy and Finance 2011/10/13).

Two factors were responsible for the Lee government's decision to renegotiate the KORUS FTA. First, compared to other major countries in East Asia, Korea recorded very high level of trade dependence on China, since China emerged Korea's number one trading partner in 2004. The outbreak of the global financial crisis in 2008 became a watershed, increasing Korea's trade dependence on China even further to 24.2% (Institute for International Trade 2012). By contrast, Korea's trade dependence on the US steadily declined, recording around 10% in 2011. Nonetheless, it was conceived undesirable for the Korean government to scale down the economic transactions with China, because most of Korean enterprises saw the rise of China not as threats but as opportunities. With ever increasing trade dependence on China, the Korean government had to devise institutional measures to diversify economic ties with other major economies. The KORUS FTA was a natural candidate to achieve this goal. Second, the policy inertia of the Korean government turned out to be an important factor. Since the Roh Moo-hyun government, Korea ambitiously launched and pushed for the major policy objectives: simultaneous promotion of bilateral FTAs and FTAs with major economies. Under the banner of the two foreign economic policies, the Roh government tried to develop Korea as the hub of global FTA networks.

The re-negotiation of the KORUS FTA brought about intense debates in Korea as to whether it would be possible for the Korean government to maintain the bal-

[7] For the concise summary of strategic effects of the KORUS FTA, see Chung (2007).

ance of interests during the re-negotiation process. While the Lee government acceded that about KW845 billion of production decline in agriculture would be unavoidable, it considered that it wouldn't be a serious problem because the Korean government prepared KW2.2 trillion of compensation package (Ministry of Strategy and Finance 2011). Rebutting the Lee government's claim, however, anti-KORUS groups bombarded a series of criticism. People's Solidarity for Participatory Democracy (PSPD) in Korea contended that the re-negotiation was lopsided in favor of the US, because the Korean government was forced to make concessions in auto industry (*Kyunghyang Daily*, 2011/12/6).

It became obvious that it would have been difficult, if not impossible, for Korea to re-negotiate the KORUS FTA from a purely economic point of view. In reality, 49.3% of survey respondents replied that the re-negotiation of the KORUS FTA was "humiliating" and tilted toward the US interests, while 38.3% said that the balance sheet of the re-negotiation was acceptable (Realmeter survey).

In the face of these concerns, the MOFAT claimed that the Korean government could manage to maintain the balance of interests, given that whereas Korea made some concessions in auto industry, it could get corresponding yields from the US in other areas such as pork and pharmaceuticals. Moreover, the MOFAT highlighted enormous economic opportunity costs because the KORUS FTA did not come into effect for 3 years and 5 months since the conclusion. Specifically, citing the report of the Korean Chamber of Commerce and Industry, the MOFAT argued that in order to minimize opportunity costs, which was estimated to reach KW1.52 trillion annually, it was absolutely necessary to speed up the re-negotiation and ratification process (MOFAT 2010/12/5). In a similar vein, the Trade Minister Kim Jong Hoon claimed that the outcome of the renegotiation was still well-balanced (MOFAT 2010).

Realizing that the focus on economic effects alone would not be persuasive, the Lee government changed its strategy to underscore the importance of economic ties and the security alliance with the United States. Facing the criticism that the outcome of the re-negotiation is likely to be in favor of the US, the Lee government ascertained that it was of paramount importance for Korea to have an FTA with the US in order to deal with the rapidly changing regional environments.[8] Despite vehement oppositions from civil activist groups and opposition parties, the Lee government presented the KORUS FTA to the National Assembly to stress that the tension in the ROK–US alliance significantly increased under the previous Roh government could be eased with the launch of the KORUS FTA.

In short, both Roh and Lee governments were unable to garner stable political support from the general public. As Fig. 7.1 shows, the public opinion sharply changed on the KORUS FTA. In particular, according to the opinion survey in July 2006, which was conducted immediately after the announcement of the KORUS FTA negotiation, 52.3% of respondents were opposed to the KORUS FTA. When

[8] In most cases, linkage strategies, either tactical or substantive linkage, are directed to foreign governments (Aggarwal and Govella 2013). By contrast, the Korean government attempted to utilize linkage strategies to deal with domestic audience.

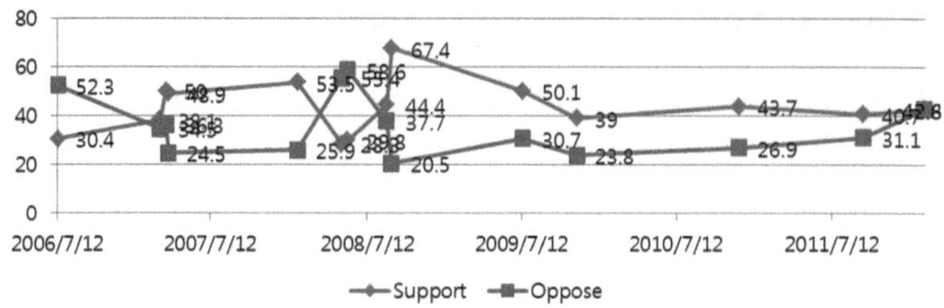

Fig. 7.1 Public opinion on the KORUS FTA in Korea. *Source:* Realmeter

the Lee Myung-bak government came to power, the general public's attitude toward the KORUS FTA was once again highly critical in the summer of 2008 as the entire Korean society was deeply divided over the importation of US beef.

In short, shifting and unfavorable political landscape prompted both Roh and Lee governments to invoke security implications of the KORUS FTA. Both governments recognized that in order to persuade the Korean people, it was not enough to focus on the economic effects of the KORUS FTA alone. Under unfavorable domestic political situation toward the KORUS FTA, both governments tried to emphasize the security externality of the KORUS FTA, arguing that the KORUS FTA would pave the way for bolstering diplomatic and security relations between the two traditional allies in a region where the balance of power was shifting due to the rise of China and the nuclear adventurism of North Korea.

The KORUS FTA has undergone the securitization process, which substantially changed the domestic political dynamics involved in the KORUS FTA negotiations. The Korean government linked security issues to the KORUS FTA because the Korean society was split over the economic benefits of the KORUS FTA. With its economic effects being dubious, the Korean government began to highlight security externality of the KORUS FTA. However, the Korean government's strategy produced unintended consequences to exacerbate the domestic division and conflicts in Korea. It was unclear to the Korean public whether by linking security issues to the FTA, Korea should (and/or could) seek more concessions from the US or sacrifice economic gains to save the alliance. Before security linkage was established, the Korean domestic society was divided mainly over the issue of economic effects of the KORUS FTA. As the Korean government resorted to the securitized nature of the KORUS FTA, ideological confrontation exacerbated between pro- and anti-KORUS FTA camps (Lee 2006a). The securitized nature of the KORUS FTA complicated the political dynamics in Korea. It is particularly true given that the general public was less critical of the Korea-EU FTA although it was modeled after the KORUS FTA and included some more sensitive issues.

7.4 Conclusion: The Politics of Path Dependence and Domestic Constraints[9]

The evolution of Korea's FTA strategy shows that the Korean government aggressively pursued changes in foreign economic policy since the late 1990s. It was the Kim Dae-jung government that embraced bilateral FTAs as a new alternative of Korea's foreign economic policy. Although FTAs emerged as a viable alternative to the existing trade policy that had focused on multilateral trade liberalization, the Kim government took a gradual approach to FTAs to manage potential opposition. The Kim government's FTA strategy was well reflected in its partner selection and scope of FTAs. The Roh Moo-hyun government combined the FTA and regional strategies. Seeking bilateral FTAs as a means to strengthen economic ties with East Asian countries, the Roh Moo-hyun government formulated the FTA strategy that could develop Korea into a regional as well as global FTA hub.

The proactive FTA strategy of the Roh government left a deep imprint both in terms of number and scope of FTAs. Korea could position itself as a regional and global FTA hub by concluding FTAs with 45 countries. Korea also signed a high quality FTA with the US, setting a standard followed by other countries. However, the success of Korea's FTA strategy brought about an unexpected outcome as the Park government was retarded in making a transition to mega FTAs in the 2010s.

The Korean government's move to mega FTAs demonstrate the way in which both the legacy of existing FTA policy and domestic constraints shaped the contours of changes in FTA strategy. In June 2013, the Park Geun-hye government unveiled the "New Trade Policy Roadmap" (Ministry of Trade, Industry and Energy 2013: 1). In contrast to previous governments that focused on concluding FTAs as many as possible, the new roadmap aimed to effectively link industrial and trade policy. For this goal, the Park government thought that it needed to streamline the policy-making process to integrate trade negotiations, implementation, and complementary measures. It was an attempt to create a symbiotic system where domestic stakeholders could share the benefits of trade liberalization (Ministry of Industry, Trade and Energy 2013: 2).

The new trade policy roadmap was based on a critical assessment of the existing trade policy, suggesting that the Korean government with fragmented trade policy-making structure could not properly address compensatory measures for victims of FTAs in a preemptive manner. It was confirmed in the interview by assistant secretary of the Ministry of Industry, Trade and Energy Choi Kyung Lim who said that although the Korean government thus far has been successful in creating the FTA network, it tended to focus on FTA negotiations themselves. The Park government assessed that because the previous governments downplayed smooth communications with the private sector, excessive social costs were incurred in implementing FTAs (Kitanet June 14, 2013).

---

[9] This section draws on Lee (2016).

The new roadmap also suggested Korea's vision for new trade architecture in East Asia. Foreseeing that China-led East Asian economies and the US-led Asia Pacific economies would form the basis of the trade architecture in the region, the roadmap stressed that Korea would attempt to play a role of linchpin in connecting the two economies.[10] It signified that the Korean government anticipated that East Asian countries would shift to mega FTAs, or the TPP and the RCEP (Institute of International Trade of Korea 2011). However, the Park government could not make a drastic change in the existing FTA strategy, making Korea retarded in shifting to mega FTAs, in particular the TPP. The Park government was tempted to complete the global FTA hub strategy by launching the Korea-China FTA negotiations as well as exclusively enjoy the economic benefits of the KORUS FTA ahead of other competing countries. The Korean government saw a drastic shift to mega FTAs premature. The Park government thought that Korea with negotiations of the KORUS FTA just completed should be able to enjoy the first move advantage before other competing countries in East Asia including Japan could conclude the TPP negotiations. The fact that Korea already secured FTAs with seven countries of the TPP participants further strengthened the Korean government's thinking that it did not have to haste joining the TPP.

Based on the optimistic anticipation, the Park government placed a higher priority on the Korea-China FTA than the TPP. The conclusion of the Korea-China FTA would mean the ultimate completion of the global FTA hub strategy, because Korea would become one of the few countries with FTAs with major economies such as the US, the EU, and China. In order to become a linchpin, the Park government thought that it was absolutely necessary to conclude the Korea-China FTA as soon as possible. Given that Korea already signed the KORUS FTA, the Korean government expected that Korea would be in a good position to link the TPP and the RCEP if Korea concluded an FTA with China (Ministry of Industry, Trade and Energy 2013).

Domestic constraints from potential political backlash to the TPP was another factor that facilitated path dependence of Korea's FTA strategy, delaying its decision about the TPP. Recalling that the previous governments of Roh and Lee suffered in negotiating and ratifying the KORUS FTA, the Park government worried that the TPP negotiations would bring about another political struggles, derailing domestic reform agendas during the initial stage of her presidential term.

References

Aggarwal, Vinod K, Mingyo Koo (eds) (2007) *Asia's new institutional architecture: evolving structures for managing trade, financial, and security relations*. Springer, Berlin/Heidelberg.

Aggarwal, Vinod K, Kristi Govella (eds) (2013) *Linking trade and security: evolving institutions and strategies in Asia, Europe, and the United States*. Springer, New York.

Baldwin, Richard. 1993. *A Domino Theory of Regionalism*. NBER Working Paper no. W4465 (September).

[10] For the strategic nature of mega FTAs in East Asia, see Lee (2016).

Blackwell, Robert D, Jennifer M. Harris (2016) *War by other means: economics and statecraft*. The Belknap Press of Harvard University Press, Cambridge, MA.
Calder, Kent, and Min Ye. 2004. Regionalism and Critical Junctures: Explaining the 'Organization Gap' in Northeast Asia. *Journal of East Asian Studies* 4 (2): 191–226.
Capling, Ann. 2008. Preferential Trade Agreements as Instruments of Foreign Policy: An Australia-Japan Free Trade Agreement and Its Implications for the Asia Pacific Region. *The Pacific Review* 21 (1): 27–43.
Chosun Daily. July 11, 2006.
Chung, Jin Young. 2007. The Security Externalities of Regional Trading Agreements: The Case of the KORUS FTA. *National Defense Studies* 50 (1): 61–80.
Feinberg, Richard. 2003. The Political Economy of United States' Free Trade Arrangements. *The World Economy* 26 (7): 1019–1040.
FTA Korea. http://fta.go.kr/main/situation/kfta/ov/.
Higgott, Richard. 2004. US Foreign Economic Policy and the Securitisation of Globalisation. *International Politics* 41: 147–175.
Institute of International Trade of Korea. 2011. The Current Status of FTA Expansion and Its Implications. *Trade Focus* 10 (19): 1–18.
Institute for International Trade (2012) Twenty years of Korea-China normalization and the future tasks of Korea's exports to China. Institute for International Trade (in Korean).
Kim, Yang Hee. 2008. A Critical Assessment of the Roh Government's NEACI Initiative. *Trends and Prospects* 74: 44–77. (in Korean).
Kita.Net 2013 The trade policy road unveiled, June 14 (in Korean).
Koo, Hae Woo. 2006. The KORUS FTA and the Strategic Circumstance in the Korean Peninsula. In *The Truth of the KORUS FTA*, ed. Inkyo Cheong. Seoul: Haenam. (in Korean).
Koo, Min Gyo. 2009. South Korea's FTA: Moving from an Emulative to a Competitive Strategy. In *Competitive Reigonalism: FTA Diffusion in the Pacific Rim*, ed. Mireya Solís, Barbara Stallings, and Saori N. Katada, 181–197. London: Palgrave.
Korea Institute for International Economic Policy (KIEP) 2005 The concept of advanced trading state. April 6 (in Korean).
Korea Institute of International Economic Policy (KIEP) 2011 Economic Effects of the KORUS FTA. KIEP, Seoul (in Korean).
Kyunghyang Daily. December 6, 2011.
Lee, Dong Hwi. 2006a. *Analysis of Major International Affairs: The Diplomatic and Security Implications of the KORUS FTA*. Seoul: Institute of Foreign Affairs and National Security. (in Korean).
Lee, Hae Young. 2006b. *A Unfamiliar Colony, The KORUS FTA*. Seoul: Maeidaei. (in Korean).
Lee, Keun. 2006c. The Political Economy of FTA: The Korean Government's Loss of Credibility and the Process of Ideological Confrontation. *World Politics* 6: 229–251. (in Korean).
Lee, Seungjoo. 2007. The Evolution of South Korea's Trade Policy and FTA. *Journal of Korean Political and Diplomatic History* 29 (1): 103–134. (in Korean).
———. 2010a. *Creating a Region? The Evolution of Free Trade Agreements in East Asia*. East Asia Institute (EAI) Security Initiative Working Paper No. 7, September 2010.
———. 2010b. The Roh Moo-hyun Government's FTA Strategy and the Korea-US FTA.: In *Foreign Policy of Korea: History and Issues*, ed. Taekyoung Hahm and Gon Namkung. Seoul: Sahoipyongron. (in Korean.)
———. 2015 Economy-security Nexus and changes in East Asian regional order. *Journal of Northeast Asian Studies* 20(4):51–76 (in Korean).
———. 2016. The Political Economy of FTAs in Northeast Asia: A South Korean Perspective. *Global Asia* 11: 119–123.
———. 2016 Institutional balancing and the politics of mega-FTAs in East Asia. *Asian Survey* 56(6):1055–1076.

Lee, Seungjoo, and Min Gyo Koo. 2006. South Korea's Multi-Track FTA Strategy: Moving from Reactive to Proactive. Presented at the 2006 Annual Meeting of the American Political Science Association, August 31–September 3, Philadelphia, PA, USA.

Lee, Seungjoo, Chung-in Moon. 2008. South Korea's regional economic cooperation policy: the evolution of adaptive strategy. In: Aggarwal, Vinod K et al (eds) *Northeast Asia: ripe for integration?* Springer, New York, pp 37–61

Ministry of Foreign Affairs and Trade of Korea (MOFAT). 2006. *Key Initiatives of Year 2006.* Seoul: The MOFAT.

Ministry of Foreign Affairs and Trade of Korea (MOFAT). 2010. *Briefing on the Results of the KORUS Renegotiations*. 12/5.

Mochizuki, Mike M. 2009. Political-Security Competition and the FTA Movement: Motivations and Consequences. In *Competitive Regionalism: FTA Diffusion in the Pacific Rim*, ed. Mireya Solis, Barbara Stallings, and Saori N. Katada, 54–73. New York: Palgrave.

Moon, Chung-in, Sang-young Rhyu. 2010. Rethinking alliance and the economy: American hegemony, path dependence, and the South Korean political economy. *International Relations of the Asia-Pacific* 10(3):441–464.

Pempel, T. J. 2006 The race to connect East Asia: an unending steeplechase. *Asian Economic Policy Review* 1(2):239–254.

Ravenhill, John. 2010. The 'New East Asian Regionalism': A Political Domino Effect. *Review of International Political Economy* 17 (2): 178–208.

Schott, Jeffrey. 2010. *Why the Korea-United States Free Trade Agreement is a Big Deal.*

Schott, Jeffrey, Inbom Choi. 2001. Free trade between Korea and the United States? Policy analyses in international economics 62. Institute for International Economics.

Sohn, Chan Hyun. 2001. Korea's FTA developments: experiences and perspectives with Chine, Japan, and the US. In: Presented at regional trading arrangements: stocktake and next steps. Trade Policy Forum, Bangkok, June 12–13.

Sohn, Yul. 2006. The International Political Economy of Korea's FTA Promotion: FTA Competition and the Dynamics of Catch-up. *World Politics* 6: 93–113. (in Korean).

Sohn, Yul, and Min Gyo Koo. 2011. Securitizing Trade: The Case of the Korea-US Free Trade Agreement. *International Relations of the Asia-Pacific* 11: 433–460.

Solís, Mireya. 2009. Japan's Competitive FTA Strategy: Commercial Opportunity versus Political Rivalry. In *Competitive Regionalism: FTA Diffusion in the Pacific Rim*, ed. Mireya Solís, Barbara Stallings, and Saori N. Katada, 198–215. London: Palgrave Macmillan.

The Ministry of Strategy and Finance. 2011. The impact of the renegotiation of the KORUS FTA. The Ministry of Strategy and Finance August 23 (in Korean).

The Ministry of Trade, Industry and Energy. 2013. Press release: the new government's new trade policy roadmap. Ministry of Trade, Industry and Energy June 14 (in Korean).

Yoo, Hyun Seok. 2002. The domestic politics of Korea-Chile FTA. *Korean Political Science Review* 36(3):198–221 (in Korean).

Kolibri 360 GmbH
Ferdinand-Jühlke-Straße 7
99095 Erfurt, Deutschland
produktsicherheit@kolibri360.de